gardencrafts

gardencrafts

Geraldine Rudge

Special Photography by Jacqui Hurst

contents

introduction 6

introduction

Craft and gardening are natural companions. Both are artistic pursuits requiring a combination of hand, eye and mind to produce pleasing results. The antithesis of faceless mass production, craft, like gardening, is organic and tactile, characterized by originality and imagination. The relationship of craft and horticulture, as this book reveals, is an enduring one spanning thousands of years from the gardens of the Egyptian pharaohs to Italian Renaissance palace grounds; from the Arts and Crafts designs of the late nineteenth century to Minimalist urban spaces.

Modern makers are stretching the boundaries of their crafts, combining traditional skills and modern technology to develop new techniques. Rural skills such as basket-making and coppice work have been given a new impetus, while materials such as slate and glass, previously employed in large-scale works, are now used more often in smaller projects. Driven by the desire for environmentally sustainable sources, makers are incorporating reclaimed materials, giving each craft a rich new vocabulary.

Gardening is about personal expression and the creating of illusion. This book acts as a source of inspiration – a book of possibilities, covering all the major garden crafts, from mainstream pursuits such as mosaic to rediscovered skills such as pebble work. Their historical origins are explored, with numerous examples of craft objects for gardens of every size and style. Practical information is given on obtaining materials and tools, and there is advice on basic techniques. Twelve achievable projects by leading makers demonstrate how to make a finished craft object. Today the garden is a focus for exciting new work, and artists and craftspeople are creating a vibrant landscape, influencing planting and design. As a gardener you are already a craftsperson – making your own garden features will enhance the style of your garden and develop your skills.

Practical, decorative and enduring, metal is one of the most versatile of materials. It can be forged – softened by heat and manipulated – or cast – poured into moulds in molten liquid form to solidify. Further decoration can be added by painting or polishing, cutting, twisting, piercing or engraving. Metal can be formed into solid, durable works of cast or wrought iron or worked into ephemeral wire traceries. An ideal garden material, metal is long-lasting, if protected from rust, non-porous and attracts a rich patina as it ages.

metal & wire

left Available in a wide range of thicknesses and strengths, wire can be bent, twisted, knotted or woven to create any number of works for the garden. **above** The daisy design and fluid lines of this wrought-iron gate have a naive charm. Made for a garden in South Africa, it shows that ironwork can look both modern and rural.

right This illustration of a medieval nobleman's garden from the *Roman de la Rose* (c. 1485) shows a metal fountain and gate.

far right The art of the blacksmith is demonstrated in this decorative wrought-iron detail. The scrollwork and symmetrical lines are the trademarks of the traditional smith.

a history of metal and wire

Metal is an umbrella term covering a diverse range of materials which include copper, lead, iron, steel, bronze, tin, zinc, aluminium and nickel. The art of metalworking is as old as the hills, and its importance throughout the ages is evident in the names given to ancient civilizations – the Bronze Age and the Iron Age – when the smelting skills involved in its production were first discovered.

Some of the grandest statements in garden history have been formed in metal: elaborate wrought-iron gates, fine statuary, fountains and urns. In the thirteenth century gardens for pleasure rather than produce were the prizes of aristocrats and monarchs. In these gardens metal ornament was rare, but bronze (which was easy to smelt) and lead were both used. Because of the difficulties involved in extracting iron, it remained a valued material until late medieval times, and was therefore used only sparingly in gardens. No actual examples of these works exist today, but in illuminated manuscripts of the time there is evidence of ornamental lead fountains, cisterns and pond linings, of bronze sculpture, and of topiary frames made of wire.

Wire too was a valuable commodity because it had to be handmade in a labour-intensive process. During this period wire was most commonly used to make chain-mail and as a lustrous thread for tapestry and embroidery, rather than in the garden.

For centuries prior to the industrial revolution blacksmiths had responsibility for the design of metalwork garden features and architectural detail. In the Middle Ages, however, their priority in Britain and in Europe was making metalwork decoration for the great cathedrals, such as Nôtre Dame in Paris and Canterbury Cathedral in Kent, and providing security for the wealthy in the form of window grilles and door hinges. By the fourteenth century, blacksmiths could move away from the forge to work with ready-made blocks of cold and sheet iron, resulting in more ornate designs. When more efficient methods of casting were developed and iron foundries were established in the next century cast iron, more durable than wrought iron, rapidly took precedence throughout Europe.

The Baroque screen at Hampton Court, near London, marked a standard of artistry and innovation that heralded a new era for blacksmithing. It was made by the Huguenot refugee Jean Tijou between 1689 and 1699 for England's king and queen, William and Mary. Tijou introduced revolutionary methods of

metalworking, including a way of embellishing forged ironwork by using sheet metal to emboss elaborate motifs such as masks and acanthus leaves; these motifs were often gilded. Under his influence blacksmithing entered a brilliant new age in England.

The seventeenth century also saw a revival of metalworking in France. Louis XIII, who worked at the forge himself, encouraged both technical and artistic development. Metalwork continued to flourish under Louis XIV, culminating in the spectacular palace and gardens at Versailles.

Before lead casting was introduced at the end of the seventeenth century, lead (which does not rust) had been used mainly as a conduit or container for water – for pipes, roofing, fonts, cisterns and fountains (the word plumber originates from the Latin word for lead, *plumbum*). Lead casting brought an increase in the manufacture of garden ornaments and the more widespread introduction of water features. Influential metalworkers, such as the Dutch sculptor Jan Van Nost, produced many different types of garden ornament including lead urns and statuary, even life-sized cows. Such items were a perfect complement to the Dutch style of formal garden favoured at the time. Funeral urns were placed in elegant settings while statues – often painted to imitate stone or marble – were placed to create elements of surprise.

With its industrial advances, the eighteenth century saw an increased use of all metals, but from the latter part of the century onwards cast iron dominated architectural and garden design. Technology made mass production possible and cast iron proved a fast and economical way to manufacture large, elaborate garden features such as gazebos, arbours and pergolas. By the mid-nineteenth century techniques were so advanced that almost anything could be copied in metal. Fountains, jardinières, statues and seating were all reproduced in cast iron, often in imitation of other materials including stone and wood. Organic motifs such as garlands, flowers and leaves were favoured as surface decorations.

The mass production of wire was another of the benefits of the industrial revolution and the fashion for wirework reached its peak during the nineteenth century. The Victorians loved it because of the intricate and ornate work that could be produced through the various techniques of plaiting, weaving and coiling; they wasted no time in making all kinds of functional and decorative objects using this adaptable and cheap new material. The rekindling of interest in flower gardens and innovations in the manufacture of conservatories (many of which were made with cast-iron frames) fuelled a passion for horticulture and plant collecting. Wirework became *de rigueur* as a useful material for making conservatory furniture, urns, hanging baskets, and for garden features resembling tiered cake stands in which groups of prize specimens were displayed. In Europe and the USA wirework remained popular until the time of the Second World War.

The positive aspects of the industrial revolution were, however, far outweighed by the social, moral and aesthetic problems created by increased technology. The Arts and Crafts Movement was founded in England by William Morris in the mid-nineteenth century, partly as a reaction to industrialization's negative effects, and to revive the worth of historic skills of the artist craftsman. Those connected with the Arts and Crafts Movement had an almost sentimental approach to garden ornament, looking back beyond the industrial revolution to the medieval period and simple country life for inspiration. Typical features of an Arts and Crafts garden employed traditional materials like stone, wood and willow, coupled with established craft skills; metal, wrought iron in particular, had a place but was used sparingly for works such as weathervanes, garden gates and railings. Architects such as C. F. A. Voysey and Charles Rennie Mackintosh designed much exterior metalwork around this time.

By the turn of the century, metalwork – with the exception of the exuberant and organic metalwork of the Art Nouveau period – was beginning to lose its appeal, possibly in reaction to the extensive use of cast-iron decoration in the previous century. Both of the world wars affected the production of iron, but the Second World War had a far greater effect. Much architectural metal was melted down for the war effort, literally clearing the way for a new aesthetic to emerge.

Modernist architecture in particular, with its simple lines, had no place for scrolls and curlicues. As Modernism loses its austere hold, decoration is once more becoming popular in architectural settings, and this in turn is influencing garden design. One example of this

far left Made of fine-grade chicken wire on a metal frame, this French jardinière in the shape of the Eiffel Tower combines patriotism with practicality.

left The mass production of ornate, cast-iron furniture was made possible by the industrial revolution. These chairs blend effortlessly with rustic wood and lush green foliage by this nasturtium-edged pathway.

below This antique pagoda lantern gives height and interest to a shady area in the garden.

is the revival of interest in the traditional skills of the blacksmith. Rather than limiting their talents to shoeing horses, many blacksmiths today can turn their hands to anything from music stands to sculpture and are equally at home in a dockside warehouse as they are at the village forge. Their work is individual, imaginative and highly contemporary and makes use of modern materials and techniques, from power hammers to oxyacetylene cutters.

right Made from wrought
iron, this arch's twisted shape
imitates and complements
the natural growth habit of
the climber twining over it.

far right The gentle curves
of this modern, wrought-iron
gate are reminiscent of
natural, organic growth, and
provide a pleasing link with
the garden beyond.

below Here a striking
garden barrier has been
achieved by cutting lengths
of copper tubing at an acute
angle and pushing them into
the ground diagonally.

metal in the garden

Metal can be sensuous and curvaceous, figurative or abstract, functional or sculptural. Cast or wrought iron is the most popular metal for garden features, though it is more susceptible to rust than others; bronze, lead, steel, copper and aluminium are all widely used too. Metal is valuable in gardens because of its strength and versatility, which allow endless permutations of form and decoration: it can be shaped into plant stands, gates, railings and screens, sculpture, furniture and garden buildings. Today there is a renaissance of interest in metalwork, inspired by examples such as Derek Jarman's garden at Dungeness in southern England, with styles that range from the formal to the informal.

When introducing metal features outdoors there are four points to consider: style, scale, situation and function. Traditional cast-iron structures are a natural complement to Victorian architecture, but can be equally effective when contrasted with steel, glass and concrete buildings. Large structures such as pergolas and gazebos can potentially dominate a garden. You need space to accommodate them and additional space to be able to admire them fully in the garden context. Solid three-dimensional pieces need to be used carefully in a small garden so that they do not overwhelm it. Conversely, in larger gardens, especially if surrounded by open landscape, metal items need to be monumental to have any impact at all.

Metalwork arches and pergolas share a specific function: they provoke curiosity by drawing in the eye, and act as a frame for a garden detail. Unlike many supports for climbing plants, metalwork arches can be as impressive in their unadorned form as they are when concealed by flowers and foliage, particularly in winter when their dark silhouettes emphasize the skeletal framework of bare branches. Arches and pergolas are also useful in giving height, although simpler structures can achieve the same effect. Obelisks and spires, for example, are elegant features in their own right, but when smothered in ivy, clematis or climbing roses they are transformed into organic sculpture. These can be made of wrought iron or sturdy wire, depending on the size of the garden, and can be grouped to form a skyline silhouette of architectural shapes to give height or a focal point to the planting scheme.

Decorative features such as weathervanes are another way of varying eye levels. The weathervane has been a firm garden favourite for centuries. No one is really sure of the origins of this art, although the earliest existing examples date from around the late seventeenth and early eighteenth centuries. Weathervanes can be made in a variety of metals and finishes, depicting myriad subjects and styles. They will elevate the humblest architectural feature, and you don't need a church spire to own one, just a lofty position: you can mount them on garden sheds, walls, or simply on poles.

Metal urns, vases and statuary are works designed to be seen, objects that add interest to, enhance or punctuate an existing composition. In formal gardens metal ornaments have traditionally been positioned along avenues, to guide the eye to a focal point where the finest work, perhaps an urn or statue, would be

displayed, following classical tradition, ideally against an azure blue sky. They were also used alone for extra emphasis and to draw the eye to the end of a walkway. A contemporary metalwork sculpture would also look equally impressive in such a dramatic setting.

Metalwork can appear heavy-handed in some garden environments. A decorative solution is the use of open ironwork screens and grilles, fences and gates, known by the eighteenth-century term of *clairvoyée*. The advantage of these constructions is that while they allow light

to pass through and permit a glimpse of what lies beyond, they are also useful in masking or dividing different areas of the garden. Another important function of metal screens is their use as frames for climbing plants. They can be constructed from a range of metals which don't necessarily require the technical skills of the artist blacksmith – lengths of fine tubular steel and even recycled tin or aluminium cans can all produce effective screens.

No garden is complete without seating, and this is the most popular use for metal in garden schemes. Metal can be used to make ornate traditional furniture, or to construct more simple linear contemporary designs; the latter are ideal for the small garden, where a solid wrought- or cast-iron structure might look too large and heavy for the available space. Seating should be positioned carefully – it is often set adrift on a patio or lawn with no real thought behind its placing. Ideally it should be surrounded by foliage, to soften any hard edges. On patios, tubs and pots can be positioned around it. Imagine an eggshell-blue metal bench and pots of silver plants and delphiniums – the seat integrating perfectly with the planting scheme. Other ways to soften solid shapes include painting the metal in a colour that harmonizes with nearby planting, or choosing a design that incorporates other materials, such as wood.

Sheet metal, which can be cut into various shapes, is another versatile medium and is a cheap and effective way of introducing the material into the garden. It can be used to make weathervanes or decorative hooks for hanging plant pots. Metal plant labels can be cut out to add interest to planting schemes – try vegetable shapes for the kitchen garden and flower shapes for the herbaceous border. Sheet metal can be finished by polishing, painting or distressing. Polished metal has a particularly lustrous surface that appears to glow when placed against lush dark greenery. On a large or small scale, polished metal will draw the eye, reflecting and reacting to light in a similar way to water or glass.

far left Recycled tin cans make up an unusual figure which will change colour with exposure to the elements and may keep the birds away too.

centre This Green Man mask appears to be growing out of the tree. As it ages the copper turns a vivid blue-green, assuming the delicate qualities of leaf and stem.

left Made by James Merran, this weathervane is perfect for a seaside garden. The copper surface is enhanced by the effects of sea spray.

metal practicalities

Flat bar steel is available from a steel stockholder. Black mild-steel flat bar, ideal for making works that need bent metal, comes in lengths of various thickness; beginners should start with a lighter 20 x 3mm (¾ x ⅒ in) bar which is flexible and easy to work. Aluminium and copper flat bar are even more flexible. Tin and thin sheet steel (20 gauge) are also good for beginners. Sheet tin can be bought from builders' merchants, or you can recycle old drinks cans and tins. Look out for reclaimed metal in skips and at scrap and salvage yards.

Metal can be shaped in a variety of ways. The working of hot metal requires advanced equipment and skills, but there are many other simpler ways of working metal, using basic tools such as a hammer, a hacksaw, an electric drill, pliers and a vice. A fine-gauge tin can be cut with strong household scissors, but a heavier gauge requires a pair of tin snips. Both make effective cut-out designs. Metals can be coated with clear varnish or enamel paints or left as they are to age naturally. When working with metal always use protective gloves, and wear goggles if using an electric drill.

wire in the garden

Current interest in recycling, and the manufacture of objects using recycled wire from countries such as South Africa and India, have fuelled a new interest in a craft material that once languished in comparative obscurity. Available in many varieties – copper or aluminium, galvanized or plastic-coated, in thick or fine gauges – wire provides many possibilities for decoration and the creation of sculptures. The finer the wire, the more flexible it is. Chicken wire is woven from galvanized wire and is therefore rust-resistant. It is also available in a range of gauges.

In the garden, wire can be used as a material for making fencing, seating and topiary frames, as well as for the more utilitarian tasks of mending and protecting. Its pliable nature means that it can be relatively easily manipulated to form almost any shape.

Fine wirework is a subtle medium. Thin-gauge wire is an excellent material for making containers, particularly hanging baskets, as it is light, requires minimal securing and allows natural drainage. Often no more than a delicate outline, fine wire almost blends into the background, though the details of its loops and twists reward a closer look.

Wirework furniture is light, durable and can be painted, as it was in Victorian times, in a colour to suit your style. Chicken wire is also a successful material for light, stacking furniture, such as garden chairs.

Its malleability makes wire and chicken wire easy to use as a material for sculpture. Birds, animals and other natural shapes are especially successful when used in a garden setting.

Fine-grade chicken wire can also be wrapped around a framework of metal, wood or a thicker-gauge wire to make figurative forms over which to train topiary. Climbing plants such as ivy and *Ipomoea* (morning glory) are ideal for this technique. For heavier, woody plants, ensure the underlying support uses sturdier wire. Topiary is

as effective in a small garden as on a country estate – a miniature form grown in a pot can add height, interest and a three-dimensional quality to the most modest town balcony.

wire practicalities

Malleable, versatile, adaptable and cheap, wire is an indispensable garden material. It is available from most good hardware outlets. The best types of wire for outdoor use are galvanized wire and chicken wire as both are resistant to rust, though they are harder to manipulate – always wear gloves for protection if you are working with chicken wire. Many makers also use recycled materials such as metal coat hangers and old telephone wire. If the work has to support any weight, then a heavy-gauge wire needs to be used. For purely decorative works a finer gauge is usually sufficient. Beginners, and especially children, should start with green garden wire, the easiest to manipulate, which can be left as it is or sprayed with enamel paint to resemble metal.

Tools required for wirework are minimal, although wire-cutters and pliers are both essential. Good results can be achieved by simply bending wire to the required shape using long-nosed pliers. Enamel car paint is the best paint to choose if you want to add colour to the wire. If you want to fix decorative details, such as cut-out metal shapes, to the wire, use epoxy resin glue.

far left Made of fine,
galvanized chicken wire over
a thicker wire framework,
this cat can be left as a
quirky sculpture or be used
as a topiary frame for a lightweight climber such as ivy.

left Thick-gauge wire gives
this simple ball-shaped plant
support a strong, eye-
catching shape even before
it is covered with climbers.

GALLERYsculpture

below This strange bird is made from the humblest of materials, recycled tin cans, and incorporates a clever mix of contrasting metals – rusted with shiny, corrugated with smooth. Combining artistry with function, its reflective body and fierce expression make it a formidable scarecrow.

above This playful metalwork canine by the artist Sophie Thompson incorporates recycled bicycle parts to striking effect. As well as providing a sculptural focal point, its sturdy construction means it will stand a certain amount of wear and tear, making it the perfect work for a family garden.

left Exposed to the elements, metal develops its own rich patina in a vivid spectrum of autumnal colours which look at home with green foliage. Here old nails, nuts and bolts have been combined to make a witty spider sculpture that appears to be descending from the branch of a tree.

above Chicken wire is an increasingly popular medium for garden sculpture and its malleable nature makes it ideal for shaping animal forms. This handsome pot-bellied pig was made by Rupert Till using fine-gauge chicken wire. The rich rust colour is achieved by red oxide treatment.

left Like an artist's sketch, this wirework lamb by Barbara Francs combines a simple outline with more solid areas, using a combination of dark and light wire. Its half-obscured position ensures that it will remain undiscovered by all but the most observant.

'Wire enables you to lift a drawing
off the page and into three dimensions'

Thomas Hill

Thomas**Hill**

wire fish

Thomas Hill is the wizard of wire. Typical of a new generation of makers, he uses mundane, inexpensive materials to create figurative sculpture and prefers the urban landscape – his studio is in east London – to the pastoral scenery that much of his subject matter inhabits.

Hill's metal menagerie stems from his childhood fascination in observing living things, and includes birds, cows, chickens, dogs and fish. He first developed an interest in working with wire while studying jewellery-making. He found the medium allowed him to combine a love of drawing with three-dimensional form and has never looked back – unlike most metal sculpture, wire can be worked quickly, echoing the spontaneity of a sketch. Looking at his work you can see that the line between it and the illustrator's pen is a very fine one indeed.

Hill's technique is simple. Wire is bent to the required form using pliers. To secure or join the ends they are either soldered or simply twisted together. Sometimes, as with this project for a jumping fish, cut metal detail is added to the outline. Here, brightly coloured discs have been cut from recycled sheet steel and painted to create the impression of fish scales. The discs catch the water's reflection and give the piece prominence in a shady environment.

Fine wirework is a subtle medium that almost blends into the background. This jumping fish, however, with its light-catching detail, rewards close observation.

materials and equipment

Pencil, paper, wire-cutters, plastic-coated wire, long-nosed pliers, broom handle, sheet metal or recycled cans, epoxy resin, enamel paints, brush, 4mm (⅛in) brass rod, metal rod or garden cane.

1 Draw the basic outline and features of the fish on a piece of paper to use as a template. The outline should be around 30cm (1ft) long.

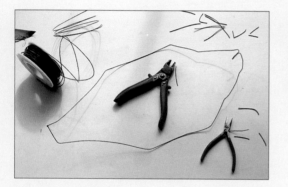

2 Twist a long piece of plastic-coated garden wire to the shape of your template using long-nosed pliers. Twist the two ends of wire together at the tail end, or bind them with a third piece of wire.

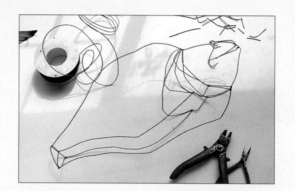

3 Take another length of wire and shape it to form the gills and mouth of the fish. Attach these to the basic outline. Fill out the 3-D shape of the body by fixing a piece of wire from gills to tail on each side.

4 Next, build up the body of the fish by attaching 'scales'. Make wire rings by wrapping wire around a broom handle, and then attach them to the framework. Make the eyes in the same way.

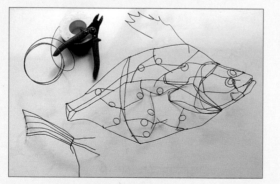

5 Add the basic shape of the top fins and tail, then add wire 'lines' to strengthen these and create structure and detail. It is easier to make the smaller, side fins off the fish and then bind them on when they are finished.

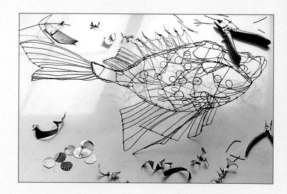

basic wire joints

a Bend the wire into a 'v' shape. **b** Cross the ends over and pull. **c** Tighten by pushing gently from side to side with your pliers.

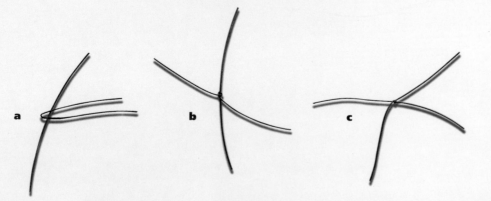

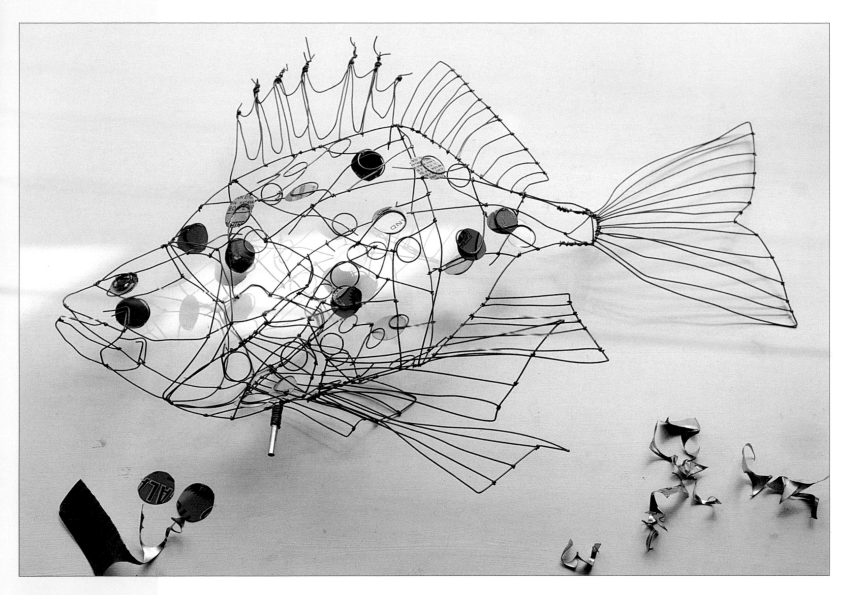

6 Cut discs out of the sheet metal or cans using kitchen scissors and slide them into the wire rings. Glue them in place with epoxy resin. Use enamel paints to create more detail in the eyes, then glue these in place in the same way. Bind the fish to a brass rod using wire and glue the join with epoxy resin.

siting and fixing

To mount the fish on to a hollow metal rod or garden cane, push the brass rod into the metal rod or make a hole in the cane. Paint the support with waterproof paint or varnish and push it into the ground, possibly near a pool. If it is secured in a flowerpot filled with concrete, it can be placed in the water itself. Alternatively, suspend the fish from a branch using nylon line. Consider the backdrop when siting the fish; if you want it to be a surprise, opt for a dark background, perhaps with foliage; to see it more clearly, go for a lighter area, such as a pale-coloured wall.

> 'Steel is the forgiving medium. You can bend it and cut it this way and that – thinking with your fingers'
>
> Jon Mills

Jon**Mills**

house sign

The perfect example of a contemporary artist blacksmith, Jon Mills is art-school trained and uses modern equipment, including power hammers and plasma cutters, to make highly individual and frequently humorous works. Mills uses mostly mild steel, forging, hammering, drilling, riveting and bending it to his will. He comes from a long tradition of metalworkers including copper bashers, a precision engineer, a jeweller and a line of blacksmiths stretching back generations. Mills is passionate about metal, describing his work as his 'true love'.

Working from a studio in Brighton, Mills makes anything from gates, railings and cupboards to candelabra – but anyone expecting barley-sugar twists and scrollwork will be disappointed. His work is defined by a passion for automata – with their cogs, wheels and mechanisms – and cartoon animation. The skills of the forge are combined seamlessly with these two distinct elements, to produce wild and often wacky works light-years away from the blacksmith's traditional repertoire.

This house sign is relatively simple to make, but it requires quite a lot of force to bend the steel for the basic structure, which is then held in shape with split pins made out of a metal bar. Here, as in many of his pieces, Mills uses different metals to produce contrasts of colour and texture – they will keep changing in appearance as they age.

Made by bending and manipulating a flat metal bar, this striking, modern house sign shows what it is possible to create using simple materials.

materials and equipment

Chalk, 2.3m (7½ft) long and 25 x 3mm (1 x ⅒in) flat metal bar, vice, drill and 6mm (¼in) bit, anvil, hammer, 2.5m (8ft) length of 3mm (⅒in) diameter metal rod, hacksaw, pliers, 45cm (1½ft) hollow metal tubing, 18 x 14 cm (7 x 5½in) sheet steel, copper or tin, tin snips, file, copper wire, enamel paints and brush, or fret saw, varnish.

1 Draw a 70cm (2¼ft) high chalk shape on the floor as a guide to the finished sign (see step 5). Secure the flat metal bar in a vice. Leaving 70cm (2¼ft) at each end, drill 15 evenly spaced 6mm (¼in) holes (these will make it easier to bend the metal). Starting at 40cm (16in) from each end of the metal bar, drill three holes at each end, 10cm (4in) apart.

2 Still using the vice, clamp the bar 70cm (2¼ft) from the end. Starting on one side, hold the bar with both hands as close to the vice as you can (the closer you get, the tighter the bend will be) and bend the bar at right angles. Repeat the process on the other side. You should then end up with a three-sided square or 'u' shape.

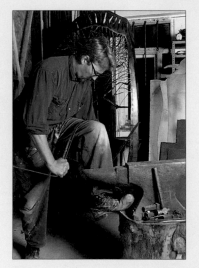

3 Remove the bar from the vice. Using an anvil and hammer (or, if you prefer, your knee) bend the middle section of the bar inwards, to make a rough 'w' shape.

4 Place the bar back into the vice and bend both outer 'arms' back down, to make the shape of a head and sloping shoulders.

5 Keep checking the outline against your chalk drawing, and adjust if it is necessary, until you are happy with the final shape. Now the three pairs of holes should be facing each other.

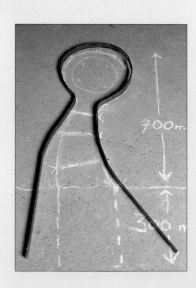

6 Hammer the split pins into the 15 drilled holes, working from the inside of the metal frame outwards, then open up the ends with pliers. Measure the gaps between the three pairs of holes in the 'legs', and cut three lengths of hollow tube to fit. Make three split pins about 4cm (1½in) longer than each tube and insert them through the holes and tubes. Part the ends with pliers while squeezing the legs together.

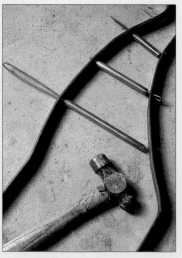

split pins

To make the 'split pins' (above), clamp the metal rod in the vice, with approximately 3.5cm (1¼in) protruding. Using a hammer, double the bar back on itself and squeeze it shut in the vice jaws. Cut off with a hacksaw. Repeat until you have 15 split pins.

7 Cut the house name or number plate out of sheet steel, copper or tin, using tin snips. File or sand off any sharp edges. Clamp the plate securely in the vice and drill four holes around the edges. Thread copper wire through the holes and twist round the framework to attach the plate. Paint the number on to the plate with enamel paint, or cut it out with a fret saw or plasma cutter. All the metalwork can be sealed with a compatible clear varnish. Alternatively, you could prime and paint it, or simply leave it to rust naturally over time.

siting and fixing

Jon Mills' highly contemporary house sign needs an equally contemporary setting. This steel structure finds sympathetic partnerships in the hard and spiky features of the natural world – pebbles, rocks, cacti and bamboo. The house sign can be fixed into position by setting it in soil, or a stronger, more permanent foundation can be made with concrete.

Strong yet fragile, glass can been blown, moulded, cut and shaped into myriad extraordinary forms. It can be flat or three-dimensional, coloured or clear, painted, etched, engraved or sandblasted. In the garden landscape glass captures, reflects and refracts light, producing the most dazzling effects. A natural complement to water, this protean substance both draws the eye and heightens the senses. Glass is being used in exciting new ways in the garden – and its potential is only just beginning to be exploited.

glass

left This sumptuous glass tile by Andrea Freeman is made of humble bottle glass, which has been melted, fused and cracked. **above** A wire spring and an iridescent blue glass marble combine to create a delightfully simple garden ornament.

a history of glass

Glass is a material we take for granted. Used to make innumerable items from test tubes and light bulbs to buildings, its origins are uncertain. The discovery that sand could be fused at a high temperature with other substances to form glass was made over 5,000 years ago. For centuries glass has had a key place in the garden for protecting tender plants. In the last 20 years or so it has been transformed into a material for garden ornament.

From about 2,500 BC the Egyptians made works of glass, including vessels and beads, by pouring molten glass into moulds. The advent of mouth-blown glass (molten glass blown through a metal pipe) in approximately 40 BC, probably in Syria, increased the rate of development and production of glass for everyday items.

The Romans valued glass highly, producing exquisite works, the most famous of which is the first-century AD Portland Vase, of cobalt-blue glass with a cameo decoration. They used glass decoratively and functionally for everything from beakers to mosaics and were the first to exploit its transparent quality by using it as window panes.

Following the fall of the Roman Empire, glass-making techniques declined in many parts of Europe. The exception, however, was in stained-glass workshops, often attached to monasteries, where glass-making continued to flourish. The use of stained glass in architecture dates back to early Christian times and was first developed in ecclesiastical settings. The earliest windows were made using wood or plaster to separate the pieces of glass and secure them in compositions. The development of lead, though no one is exactly sure when, gave early glass-makers more flexibility and allowed a greater freedom of expression. By the Middle Ages this resulted in coloured and painted windows of great beauty in churches and cathedrals throughout Europe.

Between the sixteenth and eighteenth centuries Venice was the most important glass-making centre in the world. Work made on the small island of Murano was characterized by brilliant colours and exquisite artistry which were achieved by using a range of techniques such as gilding (the application of gold surface decoration), millefiori (coloured glass rods cut and arranged to form mosaic-like compositions), enamelling (the use of metal oxides to colour glass) and diamond-point engraving (used to produce intricate and decorative designs). Venetian works were both exported and copied widely and the *façon de Venise* (Venetian style) was much in demand all over Europe. Venetian glass-makers travelled, carrying their knowledge and expertise to other European destinations, including France and Britain.

In the Americas in the sixteenth century the glass industry was slower to evolve. First attempts to make glass in Mexico in the early part of the century ended in failure, and later attempts in Salem and Philadelphia, and by the Dutch in New York, were equally unsuccessful.

In Britain, the influx of glass-makers from the sixteenth century onwards and the development of industrial processes led to the establishment of a thriving glass industry. But it was the development of cut and engraved lead crystal in the seventeenth century by George Ravencroft that brought British glass to the attention of the world.

By the end of the century glass was being manufactured at centres throughout Europe and makers were applying their own styles and techniques to a variety of mass-produced glassware from jugs and bowls to stemmed glasses. By the eighteenth century German craftsmen had established glassworks in America.

far left This blown-glass bottle, sealed with a merchant's mark and dated 1698, was made using skills that had been developed in the second half of the first century BC.

left An early thirteenth-century stained-glass window, depicting the Parable of the Sower in Canterbury Cathedral, demonstrates the sophisticated art of the stained-glass makers of that time – the landscape is exquisitely detailed.

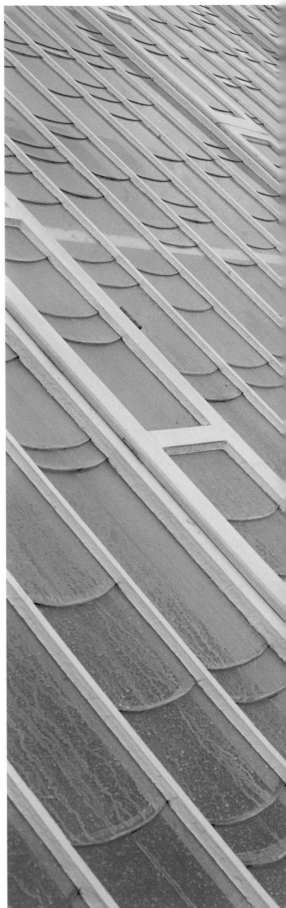

The first use of glass in a garden setting came in the sixteenth century with the introduction of the orangery or stove house (so called because of the heat required to protect plants such as oranges and pomegranates from inclement winters). These structures were heated with pans of charcoal or by furnaces – warmth more than light was the priority, unlike the predominantly glass greenhouses and conservatories that followed. Surviving eighteenth-century orangeries can be found at Wye House in Maryland, USA and at Chatsworth in Derbyshire.

In the mid-nineteenth century improved techniques for manufacturing sheet glass resulted in garden buildings of wood or cast iron and glass rapidly gaining popularity throughout Europe and America. The industrial revolution provided the cast-iron framework for glass structures on the grandest scale. An early example is the Jardin des Plantes in Paris, begun in 1833. In England the abolition of the glass tax, an excise duty on glass, and the window tax, which had limited the number of windows permitted in buildings, led within five years to the building of the most famous and influential glass structure of them all – the Crystal Palace in London, originally designed to house the Great Exhibition of 1851, for which Birmingham glass-makers produced 300,000 panes of glass.

In their passion for plants, the Victorians sent collectors to search for new specimens across the world. They built conservatories and greenhouses,

embellished with stained glass, to cultivate and exhibit the latest arrivals. Glass became an integral and highly fashionable element of garden design – such was the status of conservatories in Victorian society that people without them would have temporary glass structures built for entertaining.

In the Victorian kitchen garden marrows, melons and other non-hardy vegetables were brought on under glass. Lantern cloches, constructed of a series of small glass panes secured in a metal framework, and bell jars were both put to good use protecting early and tender varieties, while clear blown-glass cylinders were used to ensure Victorian cucumbers grew long and straight. Much in use in the nineteenth and early twentieth centuries, these fragile and expensive items were supplanted by cheap, mass-produced alternatives and went on to become highly collectable.

In 1962 a seminar at the University of Wisconsin, USA revolutionized glass-making. A way was found of melting it in a small furnace which meant that glass, previously confined to factory production, could be made by an individual maker in a studio. It resulted in the setting up of numerous glass courses and the evolution of glass-making as a studio craft internationally. Experimentation with different techniques has led to the rapid development of glass work, and contemporary makers combine new and old methods, often incorporating recycled glass.

far left Lantern cloches of leaded glass and blown-glass bell jars were popular in Victorian times and beyond for protecting plants.

left The roof of a restored nineteenth-century hothouse, designed by Joseph Paxton, in the gardens of Heligan in Cornwall uses overlapping panes of glass.

right Supported by a strong wooden framework, the lead lines of this stained-glass dome are intentionally curvaceous. The sparingly used coloured glass evokes leaves and buds, and will cast colourful patches of light on the ground below.

centre Stylized outlines of leaves are echoed in the curve of the glass lines in this cast glass design by Anne Smyth.

far right David Pearl's panel is made of fragments of antique glass. The irregular surfaces blur and distort the foliage in the background, which becomes part of the composition.

glass in the garden

Glass is an ideal material for use in the garden since it withstands the ravages of time well. Gardeners may shy away from glass for fear that it is too fragile, but it is no more delicate than terracotta and stands up well to extremes of temperature. Traditionally its role in the garden has been strictly functional and often architectural – flat glass for cold frames and greenhouses, blown glass for cloches. New and exciting techniques are constantly being developed, combining the functional with the ornamental, using flat, blown and recycled glass.

Flat glass has a chameleon-like quality. The same basic material is available in a vivid spectrum of colours and its surface can be decorated with almost any design by sandblasting, etching, engraving or painting, resulting in a finish that may be clear or opaque, rough or smooth, shiny or dull. Its most popular use is for stained-glass designs, where it is cut into shapes, arranged and then secured with leading.

Stained glass is the ideal material for screens and, unlike hedges, walls and solid fencing, a screen forms an effective barrier while still allowing light to filter through. In the gardens of Victorian or Edwardian houses stained-glass screens are naturally in keeping with the architecture. They are also useful on roof terraces and balconies, as they form airy boundaries that still provide a measure of privacy. A glass screen should be fixed to solid uprights of metal, masonry or wood sunk into the ground to prevent damage by wind or accident. Small, portable screens can be positioned to enhance or conceal different areas of the garden at different times of the year. They should be framed in metal with two long metal uprights to secure the frame in the ground.

A simple but striking geometric screen can be made using different-coloured glass squares that have been carefully chosen to emphasize or contrast with the surrounding plants. For example, vivid red glass will shine out behind a planting scheme in cool whites, silvers and blues or, conversely, a splash of palest pink will soften the effect of a red border. The combinations are endless, but you could try the tall ornamental zebra grass (*Miscanthus sinensis* 'Zebrinus'), with its bold, creamy yellow stripe, against a screen of acid yellow and burgundy, or a Japanese maple (*Acer palmatum*) with its delicate red foliage set against a sugar-pink and pale green patchwork of clear glass.

For an alternative to coloured glass, you can create a screen with clear, toughened sheet glass, using etching, sandblasting or engraving to enliven the surface. For a subtle, decorative effect, items gathered from the garden can be pressed between two sheets of glass – try incorporating feathers, leaves with beautiful shapes and colours such as those of Virginia creeper (*Parthenocissus quinquefolia*), seed pods such as honesty (*Lunaria annua*), dried flowers or ferns. These screens should be secured in the same way as a stained-glass screen, or can be placed on patios, terraces and roof gardens throughout the spring and summer. Unless they have been sealed with lead-light cement, bring them inside over the winter.

Flat glass can also be used to make three-dimensional works for the garden. A basic glass lantern is simply four pieces of flat glass secured with leading and painted with a design. Soft, diffused light filtered through coloured glass is the perfect accompaniment to a warm summer evening spent relaxing outside. The Victorians used the same construction on a larger scale for glass lanterns to encourage early salad crops.

As glass reflects light, it is indispensable for enlivening shady or dull areas of the garden, roof garden or conservatory. It also responds to the changing elements, glinting in sun or rain – it is a material of contemplation and reflection, which makes it ideal for mobiles. The humblest pieces of coloured glass are capable of making an effective display. Suspended on fishing line in small groups of varying length and hung where they catch the

light, ideally from the branches of a tree, small pieces of glass, will create movement, diffuse light, cast colourful shadows and fill the air with chimes as they move in the wind. Their jewel-like quality is only intensified by frost or rain.

Recycling plays a part in almost all garden crafts and glass is no exception. Cheap and in plentiful supply, old glass bottles have many uses. Carefully chosen coloured bottles can simply be attached by

far left The stark geometric shape of this moulded glass fountain is enlivened by the constant play of water.

centre This glass installation is made of etched and moulded glass suspended on metal frames, creating the illusion that the glass panels are billowing in the breeze.

left *Tepee*, made by the Canadian glass artist Steve Tobin, is a tall, shimmering structure made of tiers of capillary tubes on a steel framework.

wire to a plain wire fence to create a fascinating textured surface. The bases, with their dimpled appearance, can be set into old table-tops or used as a decorative detail around the edge of a pond. Bottle bases can also be used to form pierced work in walls. Arranged in a variety of designs such as diamonds or circles, areas of glass will effectively break up expanses of brick or concrete, allowing light to pass through. In this way they are similar to

ready-made glass bricks which are an equally effective but less dense alternative to clay bricks. Glass bricks are ideal in small gardens where they can create an illusion of space as light is diffused through them. When used to build small walls in the garden, glass bricks make useful screens. They also look good incorporated into existing structures of brick or concrete as they will allow light through, adding a new dimension.

Glass sculpture, from the most sinuous to ultra-angular, is a new addition to the repertoire of garden ornament. Most contemporary works tend to be abstract and therefore need to be placed with care in a traditional garden setting. The most successful garden pieces tend to be bluish or greenish in colour or transparent. The ideal environment for these works would be a modern space, with gravel or decking and a 'less is more' aesthetic.

right *Wave in a Seascape*, a fused glass scupture by Sandy Schofield, makes the most of the characteristics shared by glass and water.

centre Light pierces the spiral form of this stained-glass fountain by Killian Schurman, casting vivid reflections on the water in the trough below.

far right This aptly named *Oyster Fan* at London's Kew Gardens is composed of layers of fused flat glass glistening in a gentle spring of water.

Glass is often at its best in or near water where the two can be used together in a variety of combinations. In many ways glass imitates water, providing a constantly changing surface that both refracts the light and provides reflections of the surrounding plants. Glass artists, sensitive to this symbiotic and dynamic relationship, are making glass fountains and mosaic pools.

A small glass pool, fed by a trickle of water, will enhance the qualities of both glass and water to shimmering effect. Sculptural glass works look particularly at home when situated in or around ponds or near running water.

A simple, immediate and cheap way to introduce glass to the garden would be to scatter iridescent glass marbles or beads at the edge of a pond, in a bowl, or anywhere water collects. Alternatively you could arrange old glass fishing floats near a water source.

glass practicalities

Glass is available from domestic glass suppliers in a wide range of finishes from clear and opaque to 'flashed glass' – clear glass on which a thin layer of colour has been applied. Toughened clear glass (needed to make a safe garden screen) can also be bought from most domestic glass suppliers. These types of glass can all be cut to size by the supplier for a small charge. Stained glass can be bought by the sheet or as offcuts from specialist outlets.

Offcuts are much cheaper than sheets and ideally suited to the beginner who will inevitably have teething problems learning to cut.

Etching and sandblasting are both popular methods of decorating glass, but as the former involves immersing glass in a solution of hydrofluoric acid, and the latter requires access to a sandblaster, they are methods limited to professional studios. You may be able to order glass etched or sandblasted from a studio. Using acid paste, however, which is available from specialist glass suppliers and simply painted on to the glass, you can achieve a similar effect to etched glass. Window glass can also be painted with glass paint in imitation of stained glass.

For working with glass, depending on the scale and complexity of the project, you will need a glass-cutter, glass pliers, a soldering iron, flux (applied to solder in order to soften it), a lead knife and lead cement plus a wooden frame to keep the composition in place while you are working on it. To frame and hold together compositions of coloured or clear flat glass, you will need lengths of lead. These come with grooves ready made in each side into which the glass can be slotted and then cemented. Most of the materials and tools required for stained-glass work are available through specialist glass suppliers. If you have problems tracking them down you could ask at your local night school.

Painting glass is the easiest of the glass techniques and the best starting point for the beginner. All you need is a piece of clear glass, a brush and some glass paint. Colour is achieved by applying either enamel paints (for transparent colours) or iron oxides (for opaque colours) with a fine brush. To fix the paint for outdoor use, the glass should be placed in a kiln. Glass-cutting takes considerable practice to perfect – make long, straight lines from edge to edge rather than cutting out a whole shape in one go. If you shatter the glass you are attempting to cut, save it to make a colourful glass mosaic. For safety reasons always wear a mask when painting glass to avoid inhaling fumes, and wear goggles when cutting glass.

top The artist Peter Freeman has transformed neon light into an art form. This installation, *Trees of Light*, was inspired by the ancient custom of tree-dressing. The dazzling colours and simple abstract forms show the spectacular potential of neon light in a garden setting.

above Simple rectangles of coloured glass have been leaded and then fixed into a solid framework. Positioned where the light will shine through, and edged with golden hop (*Humulus lupulus* 'Aureus'), this panel makes a colourful and original garden screen.

centre left These thin, pale yellow glass tubes, rising like slim towers from the tangled foliage below, are a highly original way to illuminate the garden at night. They successfully combine function and decoration in a colour that echoes some of the nearby plants.

left Fixed to a garden cane, the curving spiral shape of Jan Truman's wire and coloured-glass bead aerial contrasts with the straight grasses in the background, and vies for attention with the colourful blooms of *Achillea millefolium* 'Lilac Beauty'.

above Coloured glass baubles can be selected in shades to complement the surrounding planting. The golden orb in the foreground reflects and intensifies the yellows and lilacs of the flowers, while the deep blue ball melts into the background. The baubles can be attached to garden canes or wire rods, or suspended on fine wire.

'Simple materials can make something eye-catching that celebrates a place in the garden.'

Myrna Gray

web of glass

'I've always been a mixed media person,' says Kent-based artist Myrna Gray, 'I like the excitement of one material sparking off another.' Gray's materials, often recycled, can be anything from bits of old wood and pebbles to lengths of bamboo and coils of second-hand wire; from these she makes a variety of works, particularly for outdoor settings. Pieces that mingle sound with visual effects, such as mobiles and wind chimes, are of special interest. Her pieces are often inspired by nature and designed to enhance the natural environment – her first mobile was made for her garden and she continues to try out new ideas there. Gray combines art and education, teaching sculpture and working as an artist-in-residence.

The web of glass project shown here is a reinterpretation of the old rural custom of tree-dressing. Gray wanted to make a work that would complement the organic beauty of the trees in her garden. When searching for a reflective, shimmering, iridescent material that would react to seasonal and atmospheric changes, she found the solution literally on the end of her nose – the lenses in her spectacles. She chose the form of a web because it has a contradictory nature – beautiful but dangerous, like glass itself. The web is straightforward to make and uses easily available materials, though the detailed wire work can be time-consuming.

This web of glass responds to the changing elements, providing year-round fascination and rising above its humble origins of wire and old spectacle lenses.

1 Draw the web shape, about 110cm (3½ft) in diameter, on a large sheet of card. Bend thick aluminium wire to make the small central circle and the outer circle. Fit thinner aluminium wire around the other pencil lines. Tape down all the wires with masking tape as you work.

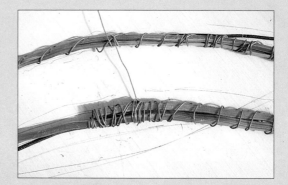

2 To make a join, overlap the ends and wrap them tightly with thin galvanized wire. Squeeze the join with pliers to flatten and tighten it. Make sure that you keep the twisted joins in line with each other and as neat as possible.

materials and equipment

Pencil, card, 5mm (¼in) and 3mm (⅛in) square aluminium wire, wire-cutters, masking tape, pliers, 0.5mm (35 gauge) galvanized wire, glass or plastic lenses, electric hand drill, thin steel drill bit, goggles, Plasticine, wooden spoon or dowel.

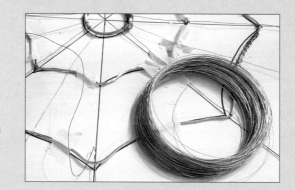

3 When all the circles of the web are in place and taped down, start to make the straight 'spokes' of thin wire that join them together. Do not remove the masking tape at this stage. Cut a length of thin wire and wrap it tightly around the outer point of the outside circle. Squeeze the end with pliers so that it does not slip. Take the wire to the next circle in and wrap it tightly as before. Continue to link the circles with the thin wire spokes until you have covered all of the drawing beneath. Remove the masking tape and hang up the web.

4 If you are using glass lenses, they need to be drilled with a diamond drill (a glass merchant or glazier may be able to do this for you). Glass lenses are heavier than plastic, but they have the advantage of making a pleasing sound when they touch in the breeze. If you prefer to use plastic lenses, you can drill them yourself. Always wear goggles when drilling and use a thin, high-speed drill bit. Cushion the lens on some Plasticine and drill gently close to one edge. Use thick lenses if possible, as thin ones can sometimes break.

wire springs

To make the wire springs for hanging the lenses, twist thin wire around the handle of a wooden spoon or a piece of dowel. Slide the lens on to the wire, then twist the wire around the hole into a loop to secure it.

5 Hang the lenses on to the web using the wire springs, twisting the wires around the web and fastening the end with pliers. The springs will allow the lenses to move in the breeze to produce a delightful visual effect.

siting and fixing

If you are hanging the web in a tree do not use wire to hang it. String, cord or thin rope is kinder to trees. Dappled shade makes the web intriguing; sunlight catches the lenses; a view behind the web enhances the piece and can be seen through the lenses if the web is hung low. Hung near a plain wall, the web casts fascinating shadows and refractions. These can also be enhanced by lighting at night, if you hang the web on a patio, for example. If you have used garden wire, you can spray paint it for a metallic or fluorescent appearance. Thin copper wire can also be wrapped on to the web; it will oxidize outside and change colour, to produce interesting effects.

'Glass allows you to paint with light
to create your own sumptuous palette.'

Sue Woolhouse

Sue**Woolhouse**

fern panels

Stained-glass artist Sue Woolhouse lives and works in the northeast of England where, in the seventh century, the earliest stained glass in Britain was made. Her first encounter with glass was during a foundation course where she was taught glass-blowing. She became fascinated with the material and started to experiment, finding a way of fusing glass into slabs, forming a perfect surface for flat decoration. Later she met stained-glass artists and, as she says, 'it changed my course. I've always seen my work as painting with light'.

Today Woolhouse works in her own studio and undertakes projects with schools and community groups alongside private commissions. She uses many techniques to change the surface of the glass including acid etching, painting and sandblasting. Her subject matter reflects her keen interest in gardening – roses, daffodils and ferns are a recurring theme in her stained glass. Woolhouse originally chose garden flora as it allowed her to bring nature indoors; more recently she has been taking glass outdoors.

In the glass panels illustrated here, the delicate structure of the fern is contrasted with a strong linear outline. Most techniques used in this project are not too difficult to learn but patience and care are essential, especially when cutting out the details of the fern shape and fixing the leading.

Hand-painted with enamel paint, framed with leading and suspended on fishing line, the beauty of the fern is enclosed in a pleasing modern composition and is intensified as the glass catches the light.

materials and equipment

Pencil, graph paper, 17 x 17cm (6½ x 6½in) glass, glass-cutter, pliers, Fablon (sticky-backed vinyl), ferns, masking tape, scalpel, enamel, acrylic or oil paint, broad brush or stencil brush, vice, length of 12mm (½in) flat lead, Stanley knife or lead knife, hammer, tacks, flux, solder, soldering iron, lead light cement, tooth-brush, talcum powder, 2mm (16 gauge) copper wire, wire wool, Zebo lead polish, shoebrush.

1 Ask a glazier to cut a piece of glass to the size you need. Alternatively, you can cut it out yourself with a glass-cutter. First draw out the shape on to graph paper. Place a piece of glass over the outline, then dip the cutting tip of the glass-cutter in oil. Cut away from you, pressing firmly and evenly. To break the glass, grip it along the cutting line with pliers, hold the glass on the other side and snap along the line. Do not try to cut all four sides in one go as the glass is likely to shatter – cut one side from edge to edge and break, then the next, and so on.

2 Cut a piece of Fablon to the size of the glass and stick it on to the glass. Take a photocopy of the fern and shade the back of the image in pencil. Tape it on to the Fablon with masking tape with the pencil side face down. Trace along the outside edge of the photocopy; the pencil will leave an outline on the Fablon. Remove the photocopy and cut carefully along the pencil line with a scalpel, removing the shape of the fern as you go so that the glass is visible underneath.

3 Paint in the fern shape on the exposed glass using enamel, acrylic or oil paint. As the paint starts to dry, mop the surface with a broad brush or stencil brush to smooth it out and add texture. Once dry, peel off the Fablon to leave the fern shape on the glass.

4 Place the length of lead in a vice. Using a Stanley or lead knife, cut four lengths to go around the panel, adding 2cm (¾in) at each end as room for error – these will be trimmed later. Mitre (cut at a 45-degree angle) one end of each piece of lead.

5 Place together two of the mitred corners and slot the glass into the existing grooves in the lead. Hammer nails or tacks against the outside edges of the glass, or put them against a straight edge to hold them in place. As you assemble the other two sides of the frame, mitre the rough ends of the lead, trimming them to size at the same time.

6 Put a little solder on the inner edge of each corner. Remove the tacks, turn over and repeat on the reverse. Push the corners together until the joins are flush, then, for a neat finish, push the outside edges of the lead together with a spoon handle. Apply lead light cement with a toothbrush to fill in the gap between the lead and the glass, fixing the glass in the frame and making it watertight. Remove excess cement with talcum powder.

siting and fixing

Once the glass has set into the frame, solder a copper hook on to the back of the panel. Clean the lead surface with wire wool and blacken with lead polish applied with a shoebrush. Use fishing wire to hang the panel in the garden – pergolas, arches and branches are all ideal locations as the panel will catch the light. Against a wall, a panel may need to be made from coloured glass so that it will stand out. Hung in a sheltered place, a couple of panels will make a pleasing noise when they touch.

Trees have been admired for their beauty and form, and valued for their practical uses, for thousands of years. In a garden context, wood has shaped and protected, given shelter and shade, formed supports for climbing plants and provided seating for quiet reflection. It has also been a source of constant inspiration for artists and craftspeople who have carved or assembled it into diverse forms, from the functional to the sculptural, or embellished it with exquisite carving for purely decorative purposes.

wood

left Washed by tides and time, reclaimed wood bears the history of its use with a rich surface texture of peeling paint and carpenters' marks. **above** This wooden letter-box with a nautical theme shows thoughtful design and detailing.

right A Flemish illustration (c. 1440) shows an arbour of wooden poles and laths supporting grapevines laden with fruit.

far right Set into an old stone wall, this arched and panelled wooden door has mellowed with age.

a history of wood

Environmentally and ecologically, trees are fundamental to our survival. On a practical level, they provide us with both fuel and shelter. Ever since settlements were first established in prehistoric times it has been wood that has fuelled the potter's kiln and the glass-maker's furnace, and whose bark has provided tannin to cure leather. Trees were also a source of dyes – elder bark produces a black dye,

alder a tawny red and the English oak a brown dye. Roots, leaves, fruits and berries from trees and other plants were also used to provide dyes. Cut and turned, wood was used to construct the first looms and spinning wheels; it provided handles for tools and weapons, building materials for boats, and simple furniture. Later it became a vehicle for decoration and sculpture. Many of our ancestors used to work with wood, and its importance is

evident in many surnames that still survive indicating occupations, such as Pitman, a saw-pit worker, or Turner and Sawyer with more obvious associations. Familiar colloquialisms, such as 'knock on wood' or 'can't see the wood for the trees', illustrate vividly the pivotal role that wood has played in everyday life through the ages.

Wood has been used to create functional and decorative garden structures since gardening was first developed as an art form. The ancient Egyptians favoured formal gardens that used wood and water, which were both rare and precious commodities, as key components. In the tomb of Rekhmra of Thebes, built in the second millennium BC, a wall-painting of a garden scene shows an enclosed space with a rectangular pool at its centre. Along three edges are planted avenues of trees, the central row being easily identifiable as date palms. In other Egyptian gardens wooden pergolas, often adorned with painted and carved designs, made a useful and decorative framework up which to train grapevines, providing both fruit and shade.

We know from surviving friezes and murals that the Romans also built architectural structures in their formal gardens, using interwoven laths in straight and curved configurations to form balustrades, arches and pergolas. However, wood was mostly used in the creation of trelliswork and other plant supports, leaving marble, stone and mosaic to be used for more decorative and sculptural applications. The Roman garden became a template for many of the garden designs that followed, in which trellis, fountains and statuary were standard features.

In the enclosed medieval garden pergolas, summerhouses, and tunnel-like trellis constructions, which were often covered with a combination of vines, roses, ivy and honeysuckle, continued to be popular, providing both shade and decoration.

Carpenters were employed to make gates, paling and wattle fences to enclose gardens and to construct animal pounds.

Between the fifteenth and seventeenth centuries Italian garden design had a great influence on the rest of Europe. Italian Renaissance gardens were designed primarily to delight the senses. Set on slopes affording fine views and cooling breezes, the gardens were dominated by water along with statues, balustrades and formal planting. Wood was used to construct elaborate galleried walks, arbours, arches and giant frames up which were trained fragrant climbing plants such as jasmine. Although early examples are known about only through written accounts and illustrations, later gardens, such as the Villa D'Este in Tivoli (1580), still survive.

In the sumptuous gardens of Nonsuch, Henry VIII's palace in Surrey, which was demolished in 1682, wood was used extensively for both functional and artistic purposes. Fences constructed to protect the formal flower beds boasted elaborate posts carved in the form of heraldic beasts bearing flags, which were gilded and painted green and white. Elsewhere in the gardens these carved and painted beasts were set on tall poles placed at regular intervals, while wooden furniture was painted in bold stripes, setting a fashion for painted and carved garden decoration that endured throughout the sixteenth century.

Another feature of the Tudor garden was wooden galleries built along the outer walls, and punctuated with places to sit. These walkways connected different areas of the dwelling with the garden beyond, often leading to a mound – an artificial hillock on which a small wooden arbour was sometimes placed, or, in the case of Nonsuch, an elaborate summerhouse. Trellis remained popular, and was often painted in the armorial colours of the owner. Topiary, too, was a frequent feature, with wooden structures constructed in the shape of birds, galleons and pyramids providing sturdy support for a wide variety of climbing plants.

right This modern wooden bridge has been sensitively executed in keeping with its surroundings. Subtle decoration combined with traditional materials and methods have produced a successful reproduction.

far right Wooden garden buildings, both formal and informal, have always been popular. This dilapidated nineteenth-century tree house is set deep in the woods.

From the sixteenth century onwards, ship-building was a major cause of deforestation – more than 2,000 trees were felled to construct an average-sized ship. Fuel for the furnaces of the industrial revolution and timber for new building programmes continued to take a high toll, while the introduction of steam-driven circular saws in the early eighteenth century led to a decline in traditional wood-craft skills and hastened the destruction of large areas of natural woodlands.

In the eighteenth century, garden furniture was the focus of exquisite artistry and craftsmanship. The ideal of the English Landscape Garden had the most enduring effect on Britain's rural surroundings. The landscape was literally remodelled: fences were replaced by the ha-ha, a raised ditch which stopped cattle from straying into gardens and provided unhindered panoramic views; trees were planted in naturalistic groups; serpentine lakes were dug; and romantic follies and wooden hermitages were constructed. Often of complex design, hermitages demanded equally elaborate furnishings. At this time the influence of Chinese and Indian culture was informing many designs. Contemporary illustrations show oriental detailing on wooden seats designed to encircle the bases of evergreen trees.

Thomas Chippendale (1718–79), who made furniture for the great houses of the day, also made work for gardens. In *The Gentleman and Cabinet Makers' Director* (1754), a catalogue of his furniture designs, he describes 'two designs for wooden garden chairs and a long seat'. He recommends an early Georgian seat with a carved shell and latticework back 'to be placed in walks at the end of avenues'. A charming chair, with a pierced and carved back depicting spades, a rake and other gardening implements framed by a decorative organic border, is described as 'proper for arbours or summerhouses'. Elsewhere there are designs for chinoiserie-style chairs suitable for 'Chinese temples'.

Dutch and English settlers in America were influenced by European garden designs, including the vogue for chinoiserie. From the 1750s onwards all things Chinese were in great demand, including garden furniture. Chippendale chinoiserie designs were particularly sought after and by the end of the eighteenth century Chippendale pieces were being made in Philadelphia.

In the nineteenth century, with its great industrial advances, wood was just one of a growing number of materials that had garden applications. Cast iron, glass, canvas or terracotta often took its place, but it was also combined with these materials in garden works. Towards the end of the century the fashion for cottage gardens ensured that rustic arbours, seats, trelliswork and staging – a tiered display for arranging plants on tiered shelves – enjoyed new popularity.

In North America, wood was a key material in folk art, used in the garden particularly for whirligigs. These figurative compositions of animals, birds and other figures, incorporating propellers as part of the design, became familiar landmarks on the rural horizon. Several nineteenth-century examples still survive. Two from New England, now in the Museum of American Folk Art, are 'Witch on a Broomstick', made of painted wood, twigs and metal, and 'Uncle Sam Riding a Bicycle', in painted wood and metal, in which the figure pedals when the wind blows, activating a double-sided flag.

Today, natural woodlands and forests across the world have been severely depleted as a result of the demands of consumer culture. Craftspeople have begun to react to the environmental and ecological issues surrounding the use of wood, and the emphasis they place on conservation, rather than decimation, of forests and woodlands has resulted in a search for alternative sources of materials and different methods of production. Wood taken from renewable sources, such as forest and thicket clearances, architectural salvage, or simply scavenged from skips, the sea-shore or storm-damaged trees, has given rise to a new breed of maker. Salvaged timber does not have the same characteristics as new wood, but it has a rich potential that makers have been quick to exploit.

wood in the garden

Wood is a natural element of the garden. It adds texture and form, and its organic nature means that it grows old gracefully. Newly cut wood fades, mellows and blends; lichens and mosses attach themselves over time, adding to the rich patina and blend of colours present in wood. Some gardeners like to observe this ageing process so much that they make space for old logs and tree stumps to enjoy the changing appearance of the decaying wood, which also attracts wildlife.

Old fence posts, rafters and planks are all excellent source material for garden furniture. For those who work with reclaimed wood it is the material itself, with the marks that have accrued over the years – the remnants of lichen, the evidence of the woodsman's axe – that suggests a piece. A different aesthetic is achieved when the tide comes in, bringing its harvest of driftwood. The smoothing and bleaching effects of sea and sand on wood give it special appeal, and peeling paint and rust marks can contribute their own beauty.

Erosion can turn wood into strange, sculptural forms, which provide inspiration to many makers.

Seating is fundamental to any garden, and the importance of providing a restful place from which to contemplate and enjoy one's surroundings has always been valued. There is a huge range of styles for wooden garden furniture, embracing everything from a simple roughly hewn log seat to a sophisticated Lutyens bench. Railway sleepers also make excellent seating and are a good way of using reclaimed wood. Whatever you choose to create, it should be sympathetic to the overall garden layout and in harmony with the architecture of the house and its interior design. There should be a sense of continuity when you gaze into your garden, not a glaring conflict of styles. In a cottage garden, for example, with its full-blown roses and wild profusion of plants, elaborate, formal carpentry would be out of place, whereas oak or log-work in the form of a bench or seats would look in keeping.

In most cases the design rules for wooden furniture are flexible. In a minimalist garden, for example, a simple, spare slatted-wood chair can be linked with other wooden design elements, such as decking, to create pleasing asymmetrical compositions. When using reclaimed wood the same principles apply. In an established garden a driftwood chair, with its worn, smoothed appearance, blends effortlessly with mature planting. On a smart city patio it becomes a piece

right An informal barrier of poles, created from ceramic but giving the illusion of wood, find a harmonious setting in this wild garden. Wooden decking adds to the natural feel.

centre This wooden crocodile, carved from a single log, rests by the lake at Parnham House, Dorset.

far right Reclaimed wood provides an environmentally friendly material for a fence. A window has been carved out in the shape of a gull.

of sculpture when surrounded by architectural plants such as phormiums or cordylines. A bench, cut and carved from a single log, can be equally effective as sculpture. In gardens which have mature trees you can build seating around them.

It is important to integrate seating into the garden. A bench or chair can be softened with the addition of arbours of curved arches, heavy with roses, which help to provide privacy, shade and scent, or by the introduction of complementary planting schemes, in containers or directly in the ground, that will grow around the legs. Try geraniums such as the clump-forming *G. cinereum* 'Ballerina' which has delicate leaves and flowers, or *Pulmonaria saccharata* with its spotted leaves and purple flowers. A backdrop of shrubbery or foliage can also be effective: mature wooden furniture is set off beautifully by the brilliant-red autumn foliage of Virginia creeper (*Parthenocissus quinquefolia*).

Architectural structures such as pergolas, arches and arbours allow a smooth transition from house to garden and provide visual variation. They are effective in punctuating the landscape: placed at the end of the garden they increase the depth of perspective, and when covered with climbing plants they provide charming organic forms. Pergolas create an illusion of space and a sense of the undiscovered. They can also be used to accentuate a particular garden ornament, although the viewer should ideally be rewarded by a very fine work after such an impressive approach. Strong linear structures are attractive in themselves, their solid geometrical compositions complementing the delicate twisting stems of climbing plants.

The standard material for plant supports, wood is used for anything from mass-produced trellises to sturdy tripods and posts for runner beans, climbing roses and other climbers. Plain posts can be elevated from the purely functional by painting or staining or the addition of finials such as cut-metal shapes, wooden spheres or even weathervanes.

Wood is a common material for fencing and is equally useful for dividing or enclosing areas within a garden. Any fence can be softened with thoughtful planting. Clematis thrives with its roots in the shade and its head in the sun and so makes an ideal climbing plant for fences. For year-round cover, choose a semi-evergreen climber such as the honeysuckle *Lonicera sempervirens*.

far left This patriotic farm gate, made of reclaimed wood and painted with the stars and stripes, recalls an American folk-art design popular in the mid-nineteenth century.

left A contemporary French gate of natural and painted wood and metal chains is more decorative than functional.

Fencing can be solid, to give privacy and seclusion, or open to allow views beyond. Picket fencing, typical of the New England garden landscape, is an ornamental rather than a functional barrier. Frequently painted white, and often with decorative fence-post tops, it makes a charming perimeter, as long as privacy is not a priority. Scalloped edges or trelliswork detail is another way to introduce decoration. Solid fences can be broken up visually by adding patterns made of wood: slats can be placed in chevron designs, diagonally or horizontally, to form strong linear compositions which can then be stained or painted to contrast with soft drifts of planting.

American in origin, decking is a natural complement to timber-clad buildings from Nashville to the Carolinas. It is versatile and reasonably priced

and has become increasingly popular as an alternative flooring for roof terraces, patios and balconies. In addition, it makes a good ground cover instead of paving or lawn, or can be used to create terraces in a sloping garden. It can be stained or painted in colours to suit nearby buildings or structures and, if treated with preservative, is both enduring and hard-wearing. New timber from renewable sources can be used; in an established landscape reclaimed wood, pitted and worn by the elements, will be in harmony with the surroundings and continues to weather and age attractively.

For those for whom the linear, minimal nature of decking holds no appeal, decorative and durable pathways can be made by sinking sawn logs into the ground. Their circular discs will successfully banish any hard lines from the garden landscape.

Wood is increasingly popular for more decorative features such as whirligigs, which get their name from the 'whirring' sound they make when the wind blows. Mounted on poles, they are useful in garden schemes for adding height and also for scaring birds, although they are often more effective as ornament than deterrent. A similar feature is a wooden weathervane.

Bird boxes, dog kennels, hen houses, dovecotes – such is our preoccupation with pets and domestic animals that these wooden structures are enjoying unprecedented popularity, allowing artists to give full rein to their creative imaginations. Animal lodgings, in general, are based on house architecture, though designs are only as limited as the imagination. Like whirligigs these works are also a popular American folk-art form, and charming examples are found throughout the USA.

wood practicalities

In general hardwoods come from broad-leaved, deciduous trees (such as oak, ash, elm, sycamore and beech), while softwoods are from coniferous trees (including pine, cedar, cypress, larch and Douglas fir). Both hardwoods and softwoods can be used to make garden features, but the key to selection is in choosing a wood that is durable, resistant to rot and comes from a renewable source. Oak and pine are always a good choice, but there are many others. Each type of wood has an

individual signature. Rosewood is fragrant and rich in colour, yew has a pronounced grain that can be used to great effect, while sycamore is creamy with a subtle decorative grain. Chosen carefully, the intrinsic beauty of the wood will enhance the appearance of garden objects and sculpture.

Timber can be bought from DIY centres or builders' merchants. The best place to buy wood, however, is directly from a saw mill. Here you can select the actual log from which your garden work will be cut. Staff at saw mills have expert knowledge of their craft and will be able to advise

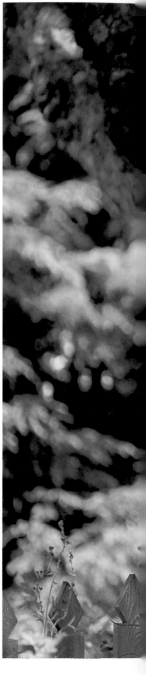

right This rustic American birdhouse by Richard Felber resembles a log cabin. It is made from blue panels of reclaimed wood.

far right A painted wooden birdhouse, complete with its own chimney and front door, finds a perfect secluded location in this shady green arbour.

left George Carter created this over-the-top kennel complete with elaborate architectural flourishes, fresh pink paintwork and gold star.

about suitability, durability and treatment (preservation). Most good outlets will cut to length if you wish, and many will also deliver.

For reclaimed wood visit architectural salvage yards, or keep an eye out for finds in skips. With driftwood, of course, it's just a question of waiting to see what comes in with the tide.

Essential tools required for woodwork include a hammer, screwdriver, saw, pliers, spirit level, chisel, plane, drill, nails, bolts, screws, waterproof wood glue and sandpaper. Take care with sharp tools, and wear goggles for sawing and sanding.

Basic carpentry skills are essential. Beginners should start with simple structures, such as a garden arch, before graduating, as their skills improve, to larger pieces such as garden furniture. A whirligig or weathervane would also be a good beginners' project. The success of any project depends on the planning stage. Always draw the design on paper first, keeping it on hand throughout, and ensure the wood is cut to size accurately.

GALLERY furniture

right Paul Anderson's bench is made of reclaimed materials. The main timbers are old fence posts complete with lichen, while the arms and back of the bench are of reclaimed steel rods and the seat is of old planks. Although these materials were originally purely functional, Anderson reveals their hidden beauty.

below Made from reclaimed planks of wood, the appeal of this work by Julie Tull lies not in the skilled carpentry, but in the selection and combination of the materials. It is perfectly suited to its location on the porch of a rustic log cabin.

above left Simple pieces of furniture cut from logs have been made for centuries by rural craftspeople. Here a wooden bench has been made from a section of tree trunk which has been cut to form a wide, comfortable seat and back rest.

above Carved from a single piece of blue gum timber, this sun-bleached bench, entitled *Twin Spirals*, is the work of Peter Adams and finds a perfect home in this seaside location. Each end has been handsomely carved into a decorative spiral shell, giving a weighty piece of wood an elegant profile.

left Made by Clive West and Johnny Woodford, this undulating wooden bench, with its light and dark surfaces and monumental ball feet, makes a strong statement. Here its curvaceous lines contrast with the predominantly angular garden design.

'Gather lots of reclaimed materials together before you start – it's like having a full palette of colours before starting a painting.'

Kristy Wyatt Smith

Kristy**WyattSmith**

outdoor cupboard

Kristy Wyatt Smith is a scavenger – from the building sites of London, where she has a studio, to the shore line of England's south coast, she searches for wood, metal, printed paper and wire. She is particularly fond of driftwood, exploiting its distressed surface, subtle coloration and smooth sea-worn edges. Her finds are transformed into decorative works from cupboards to chairs, often with moving parts and always possessing great charm.

Wyatt Smith trained as an illustrator but, frustrated by working in two dimensions, she began to experiment with three. A trip to India opened her eyes to the extraordinary ingenuity displayed in works made of recycled materials. It was this experience, together with a training course in wood, that completed her metamorphosis into a maker of decorative furniture. Many of her pieces now incorporate moving parts, hand- or wind- operated, which bring to life her illustrated cast of characters, ranging from race horses to angels.

This outdoor cupboard can be made from scratch or customized from a junk-shop cupboard. Here, wood and found objects are contrasted with the delicate qualities of cut tin. The amount of decoration and wooden details added to the cupboard can be adapted to suit different levels of woodworking expertise.

Made entirely from materials found in skips and on building sites, this outdoor cupboard is a shining example of creative salvage.

materials and equipment

Junk-shop cupboard
or materials for making
your own, driftwood or
reclaimed planks and posts,
coping saw, biscuit jointer,
compressed beech pieces,
wood glue, panel pins,
small clamps, stiff paper
or card, pencil, sheet of
tin, tin snips, drill, hammer,
acrylic paints and brush,
clear varnish, round-nosed
pliers, 2mm (1⁄16in) wire rod.

1 If you prefer, make your
own cupboard, with
dimensions of about 85 x
47 x 28cm (34 x 19 x 11in),
using reclaimed wood.
Alternatively, buy an old
cupboard at a junk shop.

2 To make the shaped
back, use driftwood or
reclaimed planks. Choose
the shape and colour to
reflect the cupboard's
appearance, and cut to size
with a coping saw. Fix the
wood to the cupboard
using a biscuit jointer to cut
matching slots where you
want the join to be. Put a
compressed beech piece
into one of the slots, and fit
it into the other, fixing it in
place with wood glue.

3 Saw the ends off larger
pieces to use as
mouldings. Wooden knobs
and finials make excellent
features. Fix them on to the
frame with panel pins and
glue, clamping them in
small clamps until the glue
has set firmly.

4 Draw a seagull head
on to stiff paper or
card and cut out. Place this
template on to a piece of
tin, draw round it, and
repeat to make the two
sides of a head. Draw three
tabs on to each piece of tin
around the top of the head,
and allow a small straight
strip at the base of the neck
for fixing. Make as many
seagull heads as you like.
Using tin snips, cut out the
shapes, including the tabs.
Drill two 1mm (1⁄32in) holes in
each base strip. Join the two
sides of each head and fold
over the tabs to keep the
sides together. Fold out the
base strips. Hammer panel
pins through the holes
in the base strips. Using
acrylics, paint the heads,
adding details such as eyes
and beaks. When dry, add
a coat of varnish.

5 To make each seagull
body, glue a small
block of driftwood on to a
larger one. Draw a wing
template on stiff paper or
card and add tabs to the
end where the wing will be
attached to the body. Draw
around the template on the
tin and cut around wing
shape and tabs. Repeat for
the second wing. Cut the
tab into three and bend the
two outer tabs around the
edge of round-nosed pliers.

6 Cut two 5cm (2in)
pieces of 2mm (1⁄16in)
wire rod and bend a 1cm
(1⁄2in) length at right angles
to the rest. Thread the long
end through the wing tabs,
then bend the other end at
right angles too. The wing
should now swing loose on
the rod. Drill two 2mm (1⁄16in)
holes in the side of the
seagull's body. Push the
ends of the wire into the
holes and use the remaining
extended tab to position the
wing at an angle.

7 Cut the legs of the seagulls from lengths of 2mm (¹⁄₁₆in) rod. Drill two holes 2mm (¹⁄₁₆in) wide and 15mm (⅝in) deep into the base of the body and push in the legs. For the flying seagull, use one long supporting rod rather than two. To position and fix the birds on the cupboard, drill 2mm (¹⁄₁₆in) holes into the top as deeply as possible, without going right through the wood, and push in the legs. Glue the birds into place once you are happy with the positioning. Adjust the angle of the wings from the body so that the wind will catch in them to provide some movement.

siting and fixing

Kristy Wyatt Smith's outdoor cupboard is a free-standing piece which makes a useful storage place in the garden and could provide a delightful focal point for a children's play area. Situate it near a wall or fence or in a sheltered area. Plants that thrive by the sea, such as sea grasses and pinks, will complement the materials if planted nearby.

'Folk art, cheap wood, good wind, bird flies – folk magic!'

Ron Fuller

goldfinch whirligig

Ron Fuller makes wind machines. In his Suffolk cottage garden, sailors' arms whirr, ducks' wings flap and propellers whizz whenever the wind blows. His passion for folk art stems from a liking for simple solutions, pleasing artistry and 'the idea that people like making things even though they've had no formal training'.

After studying fine art, Fuller started to make simple wooden toys in his early twenties but, being mechanically minded with a wry sense of humour, these were soon transformed by cranks, wheels and simple mechanisms into automata. Today he uses a variety of mechanisms, from electronic circuits and radio-control to wind power, to achieve the required effect. One of his latest automata is a typical tongue-in-cheek comment on current craft practice. He calls it *Driftwood's Revenge* as it features a craftsman being hanged because he's used too much driftwood in his work.

Fuller was first introduced to whirligigs, a popular feature of rural gardens and farms, by his father, and has ensured they are once more a popular feature of the rural Suffolk skyline. He often chooses garden birds or ducks as his subjects. The goldfinch whirligig shown here can be made with fairly basic woodworking skills – though the wings require some care to ensure they are made accurately.

This goldfinch whirligig is made of plywood and softwood. Situated in a windy spot, its wings will spin enthusiastically.

materials and equipment

Stiff paper or card, pencil, scissors, 15 x 10 x 1cm (6 x 4 x ¼in) sheet of plywood, vice, coping saw, sandpaper, drill, two 15 x 2 x 1.5cm (6 x ¾ x ½in) pieces of softwood, Stanley knife, nail, white

acrylic primer and brush, acrylic paints, two 2cm (¾in) and one 7cm (2¾in) brass rods – interior diameter 3.2mm (⅛in), two washers, soldering iron and copper wire, or 3.2 starlock washers, 15–20cm (6–8in) brass rod – outside diameter 3.2mm (⅛in).

1 Draw a bird shape, about 15cm (6in) long, on stiff paper or card, and cut it out. Draw around it on a piece of plywood. Make a pencil mark in the very centre of the shape to indicate where to drill a hole for the wings.

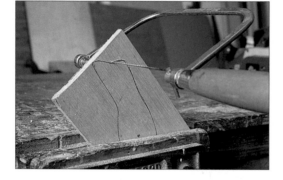

2 Clamp the plywood in a vice and cut around the shape with a coping saw. Smooth the edges of the cut-out shape with sandpaper. Drill a hole in the middle of the shape, about 4mm (¼in) in diameter.

3 To make the wings, or propellers, mark out where to cut in pencil. Draw a central line around the middle, then add a line on either side about 1.5cm (⅝in) away. Draw diagonals as indicated (right), then straight lines 3mm (⅒in) from the diagonal to each end.

4 Clamp the wood in a vice and cut to the lines with a Stanley knife or a coping saw. You are aiming to create a carved shape with a twist so that one end is at right angles to the other. Drill a hole, 4mm (³⁄₁₆in) in diameter, in the central section of each wing. Smooth any rough edges with sandpaper. Put a nail through the hole and hold lightly between the thumb and forefinger to check that the propeller is evenly balanced. If not, sand again until it is.

5 Apply a coat of white acrylic primer before painting the colours on to the wood of the body and wings. The top colours can be as abstract or as realistic as you want. When you have finished, apply a coat of varnish to protect the surface.

6 To fix the wings on to the bird, insert a short brass tube into each wing hole. Thread a longer brass tube through the body of the bird, placing a washer on each side of the body. Slide on the wings and secure by soldering soft copper wire on to the ends, or use 3.2 starlock washers, available in model or craft shops.

siting and fixing

Ron Fuller's goldfinch whirligig adds height and interest to any garden landscape. Fix the finished bird on to a 15–20cm (6–8in) brass rod by drilling a hole into the bird's body and pushing in the rod – add epoxy resin glue if necessary. The rod can then be fixed to a fence or post, or almost any garden structure. For city dwellers without a garden it will work equally well if attached to a window-box. For the most dynamic results it should always be positioned at right angles to the prevailing wind.

Willow and coppice wood are traditional materials that have been harvested since the time of the first flint axe. Willow is light, flexible and frequently woven, while coppiced wood tends to be more solid and durable. They are often used together, bringing a sense of the rural past to our largely urban lives. On their own or combined, they can be used to form organic garden structures that are both useful and ornamental, from fences, screens, gates and furniture to abstract and figurative sculptural forms.

willow & coppice wood

left Strong, flexible and easy to work, willow has been used in garden structures for centuries to make everything from arbours to trelliswork. **above** The traditional bee skep of woven brown willow softened by wild strawberries completes a rustic scene.

a history of willow and coppice wood

A coppice is an area of a wood that consists of undergrowth and small trees; coppicing, a form of woodland management that has been practised for over 5,000 years, is the cutting of shoots and branches in rotation, allowing time between harvests for new shoots to develop. Depending on the type of wood, the length of the felling cycle can be anything between one and 25 years. As a term, coppice wood can be applied to any broad-leaved, deciduous, hardwood tree that readily produces new growth after cutting. Coppicing is beneficial on all counts – trees are rejuvenated, new shoots develop and the woodland floor benefits from the increased light after a felling. Previously dormant plants that were unable to germinate or produce growth due to the shade cast by the tree canopy spring to life again. A wide variety of trees can be successfully coppiced – from hazel, which makes excellent pea sticks and beanpoles, to lime, alder, yew, sycamore, sweet chestnut, oak and birch.

Since the beginning of the industrial revolution, the word coppice, when applied to furniture and woodwork, has come to mean anything that is fashioned in a rustic style. Although furniture made of coppice wood can be elaborately worked, it is in the rustic sense that it is used here. Willow is technically a type of coppice wood but, because it is produced in long, straight shoots rather than the branch-and-twig constructions more commonly associated with the term, it is treated separately here. All types of willow can be coppiced, even

right This willow cathedral was made in 1792 to test the theory that Gothic architecture was inspired by earlier wattle structures.

white willow (*Salix alba*) and crack willow (*S. fragilis*), both of which can grow to a huge size.

The derivation of the word willow is uncertain, but it is known to be one of the oldest in the English language. One suggestion is that it comes from the Anglo-Saxon *welig*, with a meaning similar to willowy. Whatever its origins, willow has long held a prominent place in folklore. In Celtic times it was valued as a sacred and a practical material. Gypsies believed it had fertility giving powers, while the Romans used it to relieve headaches and fevers long before the invention of aspirin (containing salicylic acid which is derived from willow).

Extremely versatile, willow has been used since early times to make utilitarian items such as containers, baskets, traps and hurdles. Given the right conditions – its natural habitat is near water – willow grows quickly and vigorously, producing a good annual harvest. In areas like the Somerset Levels, where most of Britain's willow has been grown for many centuries, the water table is high, providing an ideal environment for osier beds to thrive. Here fragments of willow baskets made in the early Iron Age have been found. North American Indian tribes had well established traditions of working with natural fibres, including willow, long before the first settlers arrived.

Although there are no existing examples of early willow work, it is likely that willow, because of its pliable qualities and prolific nature, has always been

left The asymmetrical shape of this arbour has been dictated by the irregular form of the wood. Elaborate twig mosaic decorates the surface.

useful in the garden for both practical and decorative purposes. Surviving illustrations and frescoes from Roman times reveal how flexible green willow was used for securing climbing plants and grapevines and as a material for weaving baskets for gathering fruit and vegetables.

In the medieval garden wood from managed coppices was widely used. Almost everyone had access to wood from coppices, from the lord of the manor to his serfs – coppice wood was an essential, providing fuel and shelter as well as the means to make furniture, tools and garden pieces. The feudal division of land through large parts of what is now

Europe resulted in a great demand for boundaries – hedges, ditches and fences – for rich and poor alike. Wattle fencing, of woven hazel or willow, and paling fences were commonly employed to secure or divide garden plots, used as edging for flower beds and as perimeters for orchards.

In the gardens of the wealthy, coppice-work arbours were an extremely fashionable garden feature. Constructed of flexible willow or hazel poles, these provided shade when covered by grapevines or other climbing plants. Coppice-work gates, trellis and pergolas were also popular in gardens of the fourteenth and fifteenth centuries.

By the eighteenth century coppice work was becoming more widespread. As perceptions of nature began to change, the regimented knot gardens and parterres of the seventeenth century began to lose favour; the over-crimped and manicured aesthetic of the formal garden was replaced in the early eighteenth century by a vision of natural beauty – the English Landscape Garden. Influenced by literature, poetry, philosophy and landscape painting, in particular views of Tivoli by Claude Lorrain and Gaspard Poussin, an idealized landscape was created which favoured classical ruins, panoramic sweeping vistas, rolling hills, serpentine lakes and copses, many of which, ironically, were man-made. As the century progressed, picturesque coppice-work hermitages, complete with resident hermits, sprang up in a variety of styles. They featured thatched roofs with decorations of twig mosaic, tree roots and sometimes bones and animal teeth. Moss and heather were used for insulation, while interiors were furnished with coppice-wood pieces. This architecture in turn spawned other coppice-work features: bridges, arbours and porches in a similar style all of a simple, crude construction.

Coppice work reached its peak in Victorian times. By the mid-nineteenth century the excesses of the industrial revolution were being challenged and a sentimental preoccupation with nature put a new emphasis on all things rustic. Untrimmed branches in decorative combinations were used for gates, fences, bridges and garden furniture. Related to the hermitage in its use of materials rather than its function, the Victorian summerhouse was often topped with thatch and decorated with designs of pine cones and other natural materials gathered from the countryside. Indoors, the rustic theme was continued with picture frames and furniture and tiered coppice-work staging for conservatories.

Willow and coppice work may have their origins in Europe, but these traditions have also developed and flourished in North America. From the beginning of the seventeenth century when Europeans began to emigrate to the New World, taking their rural skills and knowledge with them, they used the natural materials that were available, adapting and developing them for their work, and gradually building a separate tradition in their new country. Coppice work would have been undertaken by early settlers as a matter of necessity, but by the nineteenth century there was a growing market for coppice-work furniture. Talented craftsmen emerged, stretching from the Appalachian Mountains in the southern States to the Adirondack Mountains in northern New York State. Given limited materials the Adirondack craftsmen showed great ingenuity in the design of their furniture. They used bark, such as silver birch, as a veneer and twig mosaic as decoration for their cedar and yellow birch pieces, sometimes incorporating reclaimed items such as fishing rods and oars. The extraordinary range of work they produced is now so famous that Adirondack has become a generic term in the USA for coppice work in general. Original pieces are now collectors' items, but the Adirondack influence is still a compelling one for the many contemporary makers of coppice-work furniture in the States.

While coppice wood, being cheap and plentiful and requiring only rudimentary skills to construct useful structures, has always survived in rural areas, the skilled makers of willow baskets, chairs and hurdles were affected far more by changing taste. The Fifties was a decade of design innovation whose advocates had little time for the homespun aesthetic of willow work. It was not until the early 1980s that a demand for organic material and forms revived, and willow started to be appreciated

far left With its generously curved back and arms, this seat has been woven from green willow and is typical of American rustic work.

left Identical coppice-work gates create a pleasing mirror image. They appear to be improvised but, as the detail shows, they are the product of thoughtful design.

again. Willow is now enjoying as much popularity as it ever did. Valued as an environmentally sustainable crop, it has attracted a new generation of international makers, particularly in the UK and North America, who often grow their own willow, as their forebears did. They frequently combine willow with other coppiced wood, and build on traditional processes to produce a new body of sculptural work, frequently for outdoor settings.

The American environmental artist Patrick Dougherty makes large-scale installations using existing trees and willow to create a woven structure of passages and tunnels – a natural adventure playground for children. Serena de la Hey, a British artist who lives and works on the Somerset Levels, uses woven willow as a medium for sculpture. Her repertoire ranges from larger-than-life figures that stride across the landscape to birds and animals, all made in the fluid lines characteristic of her style.

far left This wigwam surrounding a small pond is made of bamboo uprights secured by brown willow which forms both the base and a decorative spiral detail curling up the structure.

left A living willow arbour provides a beautiful garden feature as well as summer shade. The flexible qualities of green willow make such structures simple to make.

willow in the garden

Willow has always been grown in gardens. It starts to shoot almost from the moment it is planted, and grows rapidly – a couple of centimetres a day in the right conditions at the height of the growing season. Its flexibility makes it ideal for creating garden structures. The most popular material is the green willow, a young willow shoot that is still full of sap and therefore flexible. There are also several types of dry willow: brown rods have a rough bark and are more durable in damp conditions; white rods (stripped brown rods) are the most popular for basketry; buff rods, which have a rich brown hue, have been boiled and peeled. The most common willows used for weaving are the purple willow (*Salix purpurea*) and *S. triandra*, while *S. viminalis* and *S. 'Bowles' Hybrid'* are thicker varieties often used as sculpture frames or uprights for furniture.

Benders, the willow-framed, yurt-shaped tents once favoured by gypsies and recently made by travellers in rural areas, make environmentally friendly summerhouses or playhouses for adults and children alike. Benders are made by planting a number of green rods into the ground and then bending them to form a series of arches. The green willow rods will shoot and grow, the leaves forming their own natural canopy. Traditionally, a bender would have been covered with thatch or animal skins to produce a more durable structure and keep out wind and rain; today canvas is the usual covering. The inside of the bender can be lined for extra insulation with brightly patterned fabrics; if you line the floor with a waterproof lining, it can be covered with old rugs and strewn with cushions to create a sumptuous bedouin-style interior.

The adventurous can experiment with more advanced garden structures. Because willow is so flexible it can be manipulated to form all kinds of shapes and details. Dry or green willow, bent or woven, can be used to make tunnels, arbours, a canopy for a bench, or playhouses for children. If you want to train plants over your structure, use dry willow. It will last on average three to five years and should be treated with a wood preservative or linseed oil once a year. Where possible willow sculpture should be brought inside over the winter. Living willow structures, if well cared for, will last much longer; they need either to be pruned once a year or the new shoots woven into the framework.

On a smaller scale, willow plant frames or wigwams can be much more elegant than nailed-together supports, and are easy to construct and just as strong. With their limited lifespan, these supports are best suited to climbing annuals, such as sweet peas or runner beans, or to lightweight perennials such as clematis or passionflower (*Passiflora*). Bent willow can also be used to make topiary frames to fit into plant pots. Covered with ivy they become small organic sculptures and can be a focal point on a balcony or even a windowsill.

Wood and willow are natural companions, and are often combined in screens, fences or furniture. Wattle hurdles are a cheap and delightful alternative to shop-bought fencing; sometimes they are woven with hazel but a finer finish is produced using willow with hazel uprights. These essentially rustic fences can work in urban environments, especially on balconies and roof terraces where they serve a dual purpose – as a windbreak and as a screen in locations where privacy is at a premium. The life of wattle hurdles is relatively short (about five or six years) but they age gracefully. Willow is also durable in damp settings and makes an excellent pond edging, where the flowing lines of the woven willow provide a natural backdrop to water plants.

left Created by artist Patrick Dougherty, this cocoon-like structure makes a fascinating and safe play-house for children.

right Bamboo domes woven together with willow act as plant supports.

far right Used skilfully, willow rods are ideal for making fluid, lifelike forms, such as this wild boar.

Willow is one of the most adaptable and accommodating of materials for creating garden statuary. Its organic, sinuous nature means that it can be shaped into all manner of forms that will blend effortlessly with the garden environment, while its texture, colour and scale can be modified according to its surroundings.

While life-sized willow figures make a strong impact in a large garden, the average-sized space demands more modest features. In strict Modernist environments or formal gardens abstract willow compositions are ideal. Sculptural basket forms, spheres, cones and so on will contribute a strong architectural dimension to a garden and introduce a subtle organic element at the same time. Contemporary woven willow furniture also has interesting sculptural qualities which can add both form and function to the modern garden.

willow practicalities

Willow is an easy material to work and the simplest constructions offer satisfying results in a relatively short time. Willow is sold in bolts. Each bolt is 91cm (3ft) in diameter, measured just above the base. Bolts come in a variety of lengths – 91cm (3ft), 122cm (4ft), 152cm (5ft) and more. They are available mainly in the areas in which they are grown, but can also be delivered elsewhere.

Green willow is only available during the winter months when the sap is down. Since they are dry, the brown, buff and white willows are available all year. All types can be bought ready treated or, if you prefer, you can strip your own brown willow to make white, or boil and strip it to make buff willow.

Before starting, ensure your rods are flexible enough to work. Brown rods need to be soaked for at least four days and then left to mellow for a

further day, while buff and white willow rods need to soak for between two and four hours. You can tell if willow is ready to work as it will bend quite readily without cracking.

To make willow work you need a sharp knife and a pair of secateurs. To strip brown willow, you need willow strippers. If you are weaving brown, buff or white willow, you will need a basket-maker's bodkin dipped in tallow for opening up the weave, and a wrapping iron to tamp it closed – both are available from specialist shops.

Beginners should start with a small basket or wigwam frame for climbing plants before graduating to larger projects. If you are creating an item using a regular weave or one that needs a firm, woven base, take time to practise your weaving technique. Experience and patience are essential to achieve the most even results.

coppice wood in the garden

One of the most satisfying aspects of coppice work is its appearance which ensures that no two pieces will ever be the same. Complete with bark and wood knots, it is already weathered and blends effortlessly in a mature garden, while in a new garden its rugged appearance makes it an immediate focal point. Work made with bark-covered branches tends to be more bulky in appearance, while items made with the bark stripped off appear lighter and more sinuous, better for smaller spaces. In the small garden coppice is best introduced through items such as window-boxes and planters, bird boxes and tables; these can be constructed from the more delicate materials from the coppice-wood palate.

Coppice work can be used to make any garden structure, but is more appropriate in some settings than others. Its natural habitat is the cottage, country or wild garden, where it makes perfect arches for rustic gates. It is also a way of bringing a breath of country air to the urban garden. One of the cheapest and most effective ways of achieving this is through wattle screens whose roughly woven surfaces add texture while providing shelter for delicate plants. The sharp, clean lines of the formal or Modernist garden contrast dramatically with the organic aesthetic of coppice-wood furniture. However, avoid using bulky structures in formal gardens where they may look too heavy.

The naive construction of coppice-work furniture is part of its appeal – the rougher the finished work, the better it looks, provided its basic function is not compromised. One of the simplest items to make is a low table with a single log as its central leg. You can decorate the table-top with a wood mosaic of short twigs in geometrical compositions – the log-cabin patchwork template, used by American settlers, is a particularly apposite design, consisting of a square made up of lines that

decrease in size towards the centre of the piece. Using different sorts of wood will add contrasting colours and textures to the basic shape.

Coppice-work garden furniture, such as benches, tables and stools, can be made with as many woods as there are trees. Its intrinsic beauty lies in the careful and imaginative choice of materials as well as the way they are arranged. When selecting wood use the natural shape of branches to suggest form.

left Constructed from whole and split pieces of coppice wood, this arbour, pierced by sunlight, creates a haven of tranquillity.

right A coppice-work archway and fence demonstrate some of the decorative effects that can be achieved with simple materials: note the fine chevron design of the fence.

far right top A pleasing mixture of curvilinear and straight elements, this rustic chair finds its ideal setting among trees and shrubs.

far right below This garden gate illustrates the intrinsic beauty of coppiced wood, showing how branches can be combined to create breathtaking compositions.

There is a long tradition of coppice-work garden buildings that have been influenced by architectural styles from around the world – from miniature cathedrals and Swiss cottages to Maori huts. There is no shortage of historical examples to use as inspiration, although such is the ephemeral nature of these structures that many once-famous examples now exist only as illustrations. Such grand structures are not, in general, practical for today's modest-sized plots, but an undistinguished or ugly garden shed or summerhouse can, with the help of coppice wood, be transformed into something far more pleasing to the eye. Outer and inner walls can be decorated with straight twigs arranged in chevrons, or horizontal and vertical areas can be juxtaposed to create a wooden mosaic. These geometrical compositions can be further embellished with the addition of pine cones.

Open-work constructions made up of crooked branches arranged in pleasing designs can produce a magical effect. This style provides a perfect design

construction, double up as a practical support for climbing plants such as honeysuckles (*Lonicera*) or Boston Ivy (*Parthenocissus tricuspidata*). They are also useful for distracting attention from or obscuring unsightly areas of the garden. In open positions they allow dappled light through while providing enough shelter to protect more delicate plants. Both twigs, with their delicate traceries, and branches, with their gnarled and sinuous forms, can be used to make open work for porches and railings and to surround door and window frames.

coppice-wood practicalities

Coppice wood ranges from small twigs to sizeable logs. The bark can either be stripped or, for a true rustic effect, left intact. Coppicing takes place in the winter before the sap rises and suitable woods include oak, ash, lime, alder, birch and hazel. If you live in the country you are in a good position to take advantage of local thicket-clearing and tree-felling, but do always ask permission before you take wood. If you live in the city try asking a local tree surgeon or the parks department. When selecting coppice wood look for interesting shapes that will influence the work rather than trying to find wood that fits strict specifications.

To make coppice-wood furniture or large structures such as arches and pergolas you need to have at least a rudimentary knowledge of carpentry in order to make the joints safely. Ideal items for the

for rustic gates, which not only provide privacy and security in an unobtrusive way but also an enticing glimpse of the world beyond. Fences can also be made, to continue the theme around the garden.

Open-work screens can be used to form a natural and organic division between one area of the garden and another and, because of their

beginner to start with include small tables or stools, bird boxes or simple plant supports. The basic tools you are likely to need include a hammer, nails, a hand saw, drills, bolts, a plane, a spirit level and wood glue, a cleaver for splitting branches and an axe for large trunks. Always use goggles when sawing or sanding.

GALLERYscreens

above Living willow shoots have been carefully planted in a criss-cross design to create a decorative organic screen. Twining round the metal framework, they will grow to form a leafy window allowing a glimpse of the vivid rudbeckia beyond.

right Made of white cedar and willow, this screen uses strong folk-art imagery. Contrasted against the green foliage, the strong silhouette resembles wrought-iron work. The design juxtaposes curved and straight elements within its structure and cleverly uses an eye motif in the top panel to tempt you into the forest beyond.

above left This exquisitely designed trellis appears to have been airbrushed on to the landscape. Made out of carefully planted living willow, it is a light, durable and extremely effective way to divide one area of the garden from another without blocking out the light.

above right The contrast of stripped and unstripped coppice creates a dramatic composition. Here branches selected for their decorative quality radiate out from the contrasting frame on which they have been nailed, creating a delicate, lacy effect. This square-framed piece is a gateway that beckons you to enter but effectively shields what lies beyond.

left Coppice wood is used here to make sympathetic and practical fencing within a wooded, wild landscape. Of traditional rustic design, its shape and form have been dictated by the branches, probably taken from the surrounding woodland. They have been thoughtfully put together with the fluid shapes in the screen complementing the rectangular design of the gate.

'Working with willow connects me
with the rhythms of the natural world.'

Lizzie Farey

Lizzie**Farey**

willow ball

Lizzie Farey's inspiration is her environment, the rugged
landscape that surrounds her workshop and home in Castle
Douglas on the Scottish borders. Like the traditional Scottish basket-makers, Farey
lives close to her materials but, unlike them, she is not interested in perfection with
its regular weaves and uniform shapes, but rather imperfection. Although she learned
traditional weaving forms, she has developed her own free-form style, a technique
that involves a random non-geometric weave, which she finds more expressive. She
combines functional basket-making with experimental pieces in a wide range of work.

Farey's materials are unexceptional – many, in fact, could be found in the average
back garden or in the hedgerows on a country walk. They include larch, dogwood,
birch, pussy willow, wild raspberry, hazel and willow, sometimes interwoven with local
heather and the fragrant bog myrtle. Farey also grows more than 20 varieties of willow
herself so that her supply is renewable. Many are grown for their brilliant hues, such
as the bluey green *Salix purpurea* 'Brittany Blue'.

This willow ball needs a strong base so that the shape holds together well. If you
are inexperienced at basket-weaving, practise making a few bases to begin with and
then choose the strongest one to make your willow ball.

The bold shape of this willow ball and the detail in its weaving mean that it is rewarding to examine the ball both from a distance and close up.

materials and equipment

Sharp knife, six stout willow rods for base stakes, 24–30 x 92cm (3ft) fine willow rods for base weavers, secateurs, 12 1.8m (6ft) rods for side stakes, big knitting needle, Vaseline, 40 x 1.8m (6ft) rods for filling the sides of the ball, paint brush, linseed oil, white spirit.

1 For the base, cut the ends off the six stout rods to make 23cm (9in) lengths. Using the knife, make a split in the centre of three stakes just long enough to thread through the other three stakes at right angles.

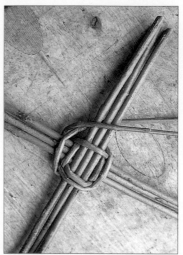

2 Take two rods of fine willow (base weavers). Sharpen the fat ends and insert into the split. Take each weaver in front of three stakes then behind three stakes. Continue in the same way until you have completed two rounds.

3 Continuing with the same pair of weavers, open up the stakes and weave in front of one stake, behind the next, until all the stakes are evenly spaced out in a star shape.

4 When you reach the end of each length of willow weaver, join in a new one, sliding the new thin end alongside the old thin end and continuing to weave. At the end of that weaver, join fat end to fat end so that you finish the base with thin ends.

5 When you have woven to the edge of the stakes, use secateurs to trim the ends of the weavers on both sides of the base. Trim the base stakes, if necessary, using a straight cut.

6 For the sides, sharpen the ends of 12 x 1.8m (6ft) rods. Dip a knitting needle in Vaseline and slide it into the gap next to one of the base stakes to ease the way for the side stake. Choose the gap to the left or right but follow suit for the rest of the stakes. Insert the thick ends of the 12 rods into the gaps that you have created. Using the knife to help you, bend the side stakes upwards where they emerge from the base.

7 To make the ball shape, take two side stakes from opposite sides and arch them up and over each other, twisting them together again and again. Continue with the other 10 side stakes, threading them through the top of the existing arches to secure them, and tucking in the ends neatly.

8 Once the basic form is complete, add in the 40 or so weavers, one at a time, by securing the thin end and curving the rod round. Weave it in and out of previous layers, ensuring that the thick end is tucked in. Trim off any ends that are sticking out. Before siting your willow ball, brush a mix of three parts linseed oil to one part white spirit on to the outside to protect it from the elements.

siting and fixing

This willow ball makes a strong visual statement so it needs to be placed in a suitably dramatic position. An ideal setting would be against a backdrop of rolling hills, or, alternatively, in an open location against the sky where the ball's strong sculptural qualities will be highlighted. To keep it in position, place some pebbles inside to weigh it down and prevent it from blowing away. Purists may prefer to tie the ball in place with flexible green willow.

'I am attracted by the natural beauty of trees, the shapes and curves of their branches, which are echoed in my work.'

Jason Griffiths

Jason**Griffiths**

wildwood bench

Jason Griffiths lives and works in the heart of the Devon countryside. An underwoodsman, he continues a tradition that has been practised in rural areas for hundreds of years. He trained originally as a carpenter and joiner, and went on to learn traditional rural skills such as the art of coppicing and of cleaving (splitting wood).

Griffiths was drawn to working with coppice wood as he preferred to work with a sustainable material rather than tropical hardwoods. Today he is self-sufficient, managing and cutting his own wood and making a range of furniture and garden structures, inspired by vernacular styles, to commission. Oak, ash, yew, sycamore, hazel, willow and sweet chestnut all have distinctive qualities and each is selected for different tasks. As he says, 'I like to use the wood in the same way it grew in nature'.

The wildwood bench, illustrated here, is made of derelict hazel coppice – the perfect choice of material for the job. The forked branches that form the fan-shaped 'comb' back have been cleverly selected to add a decorative element to this sturdy, rustic structure, and are a perfect illustration of Griffiths' philosophy. Basic woodwork skills are needed for assembling the bench; more skill and practice are needed when choosing pieces of wood to judge which will achieve the most harmonious effect.

This wildwood bench is influenced by vernacular styles. The seat could be made from small logs rather than split wood if desired.

materials and equipment

Hazel wood, 15cm (6in) pieces of oak (or dowel), vice, 16mm (⅝in) diameter hollow metal tube, saw, hammer, drill, 5 curved outer pieces of log, plane or circular sander, axe, chisel, metal nails.

1 If you are cutting your own wood, cut as close to the ground as possible using an angled cut. Take time to find the best pieces of wood – sturdy ones for the main framework and interesting shapes for the back.

2 Use a combination of wooden pegs (known as 'tree nails') and metal nails to make the bench. If you plan to use your own wooden pegs, you will need to make them. One way of doing this is by clamping a hollow metal tube in a vice and hammering a piece of oak, slightly wider than the tube, into the hole. The outer sections of wood will split off, leaving a wooden peg behind. Alternatively, you can use lengths of wooden dowelling for the pegs.

3 Make the legs of the bench first. The rear legs, about 1m (3ft 3in) tall, should extend about 50cm (20in) higher than the seat level, to act as a support for the back 'comb'. Fix the horizontal supports (4 around the base, 4 just below seat level) using wooden pegs.

4 To use the wooden pegs, drill a hole to fit the dimensions of the peg, then hammer it in as far as possible. Fix on the arms using pegs to attach them to the back legs, and then to the tops of the front legs.

5 Make the seat. Take the 5 outer pieces of wood. Plane or sand with a circular sander until the flat side is smooth. Place each piece on the bench, bark side down, and mark out where it touches the horizontal supports. Chop out a section around each mark with an axe or hammer to make two grooves that will rest on the frame. You will also need to make two grooves in the outermost pieces, so they they will sit snugly against the bench legs. Position the planks on the bench frame and hammer them in place with nails.

6 Fix the back 'comb' (support) in place with metal nails. Once everything is secure, saw all the wooden pegs and ends of wood flush with the frame. Sand down any raw edges.

siting and fixing

Jason Griffiths' sturdy coppice-work bench of gnarled, lichen-speckled wood is ideal for a cottage garden where it will blend naturally with its surroundings. Set it against a pink climbing rose, such as *Rosa glauca*, fringed with banks of pink *Penstemon* 'Alice Hindley' and frothy white *Gypsophila paniculata*. If oiled annually or taken inside for the winter the bench will last for years.

Mosaic is the most sumptuous of all craft forms. Its jewel-like colours, which include silver and gold leaf, make this a medium that adds opulence to all it touches. In practical terms mosaic is simply small squares, known as tesserae, of ceramic, marble or glass cemented together to form surface decoration, but in creative hands mosaic can form exquisite compositions. An astonishingly adaptable craft medium, mosaic will add colour and texture to any garden design, from the formal to the avant-garde.

mosaic

left Rendered in mosaic, the simplest design is effective. The success of this piece lies in the rich, reflective finish of the tesserae and the way they have been arranged to emphasize the flow of the pattern. **above** Rebecca Newnham has used gold and silver mirror mosaic to gild the surface of these two decorative columns, giving them an extravagant finish.

a history of mosaic

Mosaic is an ancient art that has been used for decorative purposes since pre-Christian times. Although it is most popularly associated with small squares of ceramic, marble or glass, mosaic can also incorporate many different materials from shells, pebbles and slate (see pages 102–109) to *objets trouvés* and semi-precious stones. The fact that so many early mosaics survive is a testament to the medium's durability. Mosaic was used in Mesopotamia in the fourth millennium BC. Examples from this period were not made using the tesserae we are familiar with today, but with small tapered plugs of coloured ceramic, pegged into place to form geometric patterns.

The ancient Greeks, from whom the word mosaic originates, produced mosaic work, but their preference was for pebbles smoothed by the sea. They also pioneered pictorial mosaic, which told a story rather than existing purely as decoration.

It was the Romans who developed and popularized mosaic as an artistic medium, extending its application from floors to ceilings, walls, fountains, furniture and pillars. They imported craftsmen from Greece who applied their skill, expertise and style to Roman courtyards and interiors throughout the Empire, using mostly stone and marble and, to a lesser degree, pieces of glass (smalti). The mosaic work excavated at Pompeii in Italy reveals a variety of styles, from simple patterns on paving and walls, made using whatever was at hand (shells or broken pieces of terracotta arranged in random patterns), to complex and sophisticated narratives taken from paintings and portraiture, to detailed abstract borders incorporating repeat motifs. The gardens of wealthy Romans frequently included decorative mosaic pavements and wall panels, along with carved stone fountains and vases, statuary and trelliswork.

The Byzantine period (fifth and sixth centuries AD) set a standard for fine mosaic work that has seldom been surpassed. Among the most famous mosaics of the era are those in Ravenna in northern Italy. The mausoleum of the Empress Gala Placidia, who died in AD 450, is a triumph of skill and artistry. The interior is almost entirely of mosaic: the ceiling, vaulted in places, is midnight blue, representing the dark night sky with its twinkling golden stars made of marble and glass tesserae; figurative compositions, pastoral scenes and still lifes depicting flora and fauna are juxtaposed with boldly coloured, geometrical designs of astonishing intricacy. Ravenna's churches also contain important works in mosaic depicting religious and historical

During the Renaissance artistic taste changed: the revival of Classicism favoured painting and grand architectural statements, and mosaic was reduced to a medium for imitating painting. The luminosity and radiance of gold and silver glass mosaic were rejected in favour of a more realistic palette, and composition and the use of fine detail followed painterly conventions. One of many imitative mosaics from this time is the *Transfiguration* by Raphael in St Peter's, Rome. As a distinct art form, mosaic went into a period of stagnation and then decline which lasted several centuries.

scenes and using precious and semi-precious stones in addition to glass, marble and stone.

By the eleventh and twelfth centuries, the spread of Christianity throughout Europe ensured that mosaic had another golden age, literally, in the form of gold and silver tesserae that were used lavishly for grand works, often stretching from floor to ceiling, in ecclesiastical settings. Outstanding examples include the monastery of Daphni in Greece and the Cappella Palatina in Palermo, Italy.

In the nineteenth century, interest in the art form revived. Mosaic fitted well into the eclectic mix of different cultures and historical periods that characterized the arts at this time. It was used for grand edifices and interiors such as the Paris Opéra, and London's Albert Memorial. Mosaic workshops were set up, the most important being in Germany, France and Italy. Nevertheless, a lot of the mosaic work was simply decorative rather than innovative.

From the mid-nineteenth century onwards the newly formed Arts and Crafts Movement generated fresh interest in craft techniques and materials and helped fuel the demand for mosaic. At the same time, fine artists began to draw inspiration from

mosaic work: Pointillists like Seurat composed canvases using small dots, while Cézanne created compositions using solid blocks of colour. With the beginnings of the Art Nouveau Movement in Europe and the USA, the medium once more became a focus for artistic expression.

While most artists and architects at the turn of the century saw mosaic as an additional decorative medium to supplement their repertoire, the master of Catalan *modernisme*, the architect Antonio Gaudí, made mosaic a primary material. Gaudí had an entirely original approach. The original twentieth-century recycler, and inspiration to many of today's artists, he used broken pots and plates, bottle glass and *objets trouvés* to create entire mosaic landscapes, such as Parque Güell in Barcelona, built between 1900 and 1914. With its decorated avenues and columns, vast staircases and undulating seating, the park gives the impression of an organic three-dimensional sculpture.

As the twentieth century progressed, mosaic became a decorative art form favoured by architects and artists throughout Europe and the USA. Gustav Klimt made mosaic murals for Josef Hoffmann's Palais Stoclet in Brussels. European artists Henri Matisse, Georges Braque and Marc Chagall all experimented with mosaic. In New York, the famous glass artist Louis Comfort Tiffany used favrile (hand-wrought) glass to make mosaic wall panels and bird-baths.

Mosaics on an altogether larger scale were being executed in Mexico. During the 1930s and 1940s artists such as Diego Rivera created gigantic murals, often using stone as mosaic, to make forceful political statements. Another artist of the Mexican Muralist Movement, Juan O'Gorman, made the mosaic façade of the Central Library at Mexico University, Mexico City – an enormous work which incorporated intricate designs influenced by events in Mexican history.

The folk artist Simon Rodia was one of the most inspirational mosaic artists of the late twentieth century. A lasting monument to his passion, and his life's work, is the Watts Towers in Los Angeles, a series of tall structures he built and covered with broken glass and tiles, bottle tops, sea shells and anything else he could find. Rodia devoted 34 years of his life to this one project, finally abandoning work in the mid-1950s, when he was 76.

Today numerous private gardens in America and Europe incorporate mosaics on a smaller scale. The British decorative artist Steven Sykes, for example, made mosaic work for his Sussex garden over a period of 20 years between the 1970s and 1990s, creating mosaic paving designs with fringed edges in imitation of rugs, three-dimensional figurative sculpture, fountains and grottoes. Currently mosaic work is characterized by a freedom of choice of materials and a huge range of forms, both two- and three-dimensional.

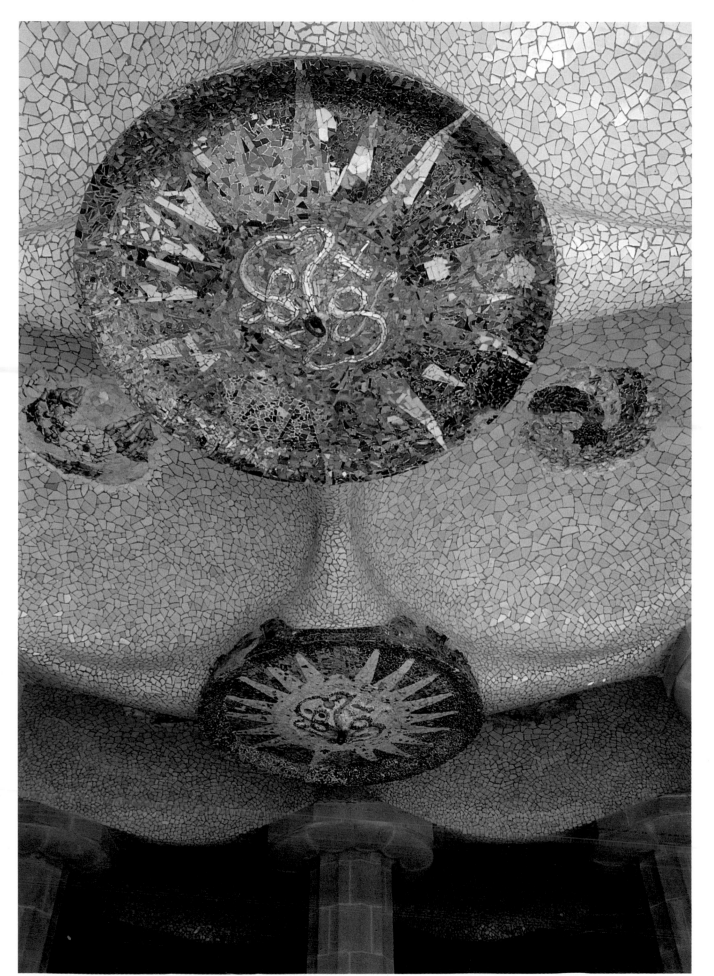

far left Antonio Gaudí's lizard's head water spout at Parque Güell in Barcelona is covered by irregularly shaped tesserae in vivid colours.

left This undulating ceiling, supported by columns, is also by Gaudí at Parque Güell. Completely covered in mosaic, it is punctuated with bold sun designs.

mosaic in the garden

Mosaic compositions, like the materials from which they are made, can be as diverse and exuberant as the imagination of their maker. This versatile art form has a chameleon-like quality, with its strengths lying in the brilliant colour palette and the lustrous, iridescent nature of the materials, as well as the sheer range of possible designs and applications. Mosaic offers the maker the means to personalize all kinds of garden objects and features. It is one of the most rewarding craft techniques for the amateur for, however simple the design, the geometric structure and the vibrancy of the materials produce pleasing results relatively quickly.

In all garden schemes care should be taken with choice of materials and colour for a mosaic. If you have an established garden with weathered stonework and mature planting, you may prefer subtly shaded tesserae and materials, such as marble or terracotta, which have a timeless quality and will blend in. In a new or more modern garden, brightly coloured mosaic in shiny or mirrored tiles will create a bold, lively effect.

Before embarking on a mosaic project, it is also worth considering the range of possible styles and where they may be most appropriate. Mosaic is as effective in a formal setting as it is in the cottage or minimalist garden, although entirely different designs may be required for each location.

In the formal garden, mosaic designs can be used to complement and emphasize the characteristic structural, serried ranks of planting. The Romans, for example, made exquisite paving using a restricted palette of black and white in bold, geometric designs for their classical gardens. Alternatively, the use of more informal pieces with undulating contours and designs incorporating fluid lines will moderate and soften the hard lines of symmetrical planting schemes.

In a cottage garden, by contrast, with its vigorous profusion of hollyhocks, roses and lavender, you can really go 'mosaic mad', using vibrant colours and bold patterns. The design and colour palette should again reflect the environment and complement the planting schemes – a series of stepping stones, perhaps, depicting fallen rose petals or lavender heads, or a design that records the wildlife visitors to the garden or marks the changing seasons.

The spare aesthetic of the Minimalist space requires a different approach again. You may think that an essentially decorative medium is inappropriate in this situation, but abstract rather than figurative compositions can be most effective when applied to paving, murals and three-dimensional works.

Mosaic produces magical effects from mundane sources such as pots, urns and other containers, large and small. A small container often looks at its best with a simple, striking design or in a limited range of colours, whereas on a larger one you can create as intricate a design as you wish. Since they are free-standing, these three-dimensional mosaic pieces can be positioned in different spots according to the mood or season, and will provide a changing focal point in the garden. In winter, when the garden is often at its least attractive, a brilliantly coloured mosaic pot, placed outside the window and filled with early spring bulbs, will present a wonderfully cheering aspect. A sumptuous summer combination might be nasturtiums in a spectrum of colours from pale lemon through to crimson, set in a mosaic pot of rich golds and oranges.

far left Found objects such as pebbles and shells, combined with shards of broken china, create contrasting textures in this folk-art inspired planter by Philip Watson.

left With its mix of light and dark, shadow and botanical imagery, the design of this textured mosaic pot by Australian Margot Knox blends perfectly with its surroundings.

above This expanse of bare wall is enlivened with a curvilinear design for both the wall basket and the mosaic beneath.

A straightforward but often stunning way to use mosaic in the garden is through paving or walls. The materials will be applied not only to a flat surface but, in many cases, to an existing one. Mosaic can be used to cover an entire path, or placed as repeat motifs from time to time to give unity to the whole path. Used in walkways and paving throughout the garden, decorative mosaic stepping stones can be an excellent way of linking different areas visually.

Small areas of mosaic paving are an interesting way of emphasizing or changing the way you look at particular garden features such as a fountain or sundial. Any design that draws the eye will be effective, such as a spiral, rays radiating out from a central point or zig-zags. Circular mosaics, with their rhythmic patterns, are ideal if you want to break up an area dominated by straight lines.

Add an element of surprise and fun by creating *trompe l'oeil* effects. You can play tricks with perspective: using geometric squares, for example, you can elongate or foreshorten a mosaic wall or paving composition to produce an illusion of space or confinement. On floors and walls in a corner or a summerhouse, mosaic can create an area with a very different feel from other parts of the garden.

Mosaic can be directly applied to a garden surface or made off-site as panels and positioned later. The latter method is ideal for those who wish to experiment with location and design. It is also useful if you are likely to move house and want to take your mosaic creations with you. The panels can be hung from a wall or, once you are happy with the location, set into a path.

Light and shade in the garden may influence your choice of mosaic materials. Iridescent mosaic will introduce colour to dull areas or enliven shady ones. Mirror mosaic and silver and gold smalti are particularly effective in these situations. Placed in shaded areas, the jewel-like squares draw the eye and, positioned carefully at angles, will catch and reflect the light. For a cheaper alternative, use broken china, particularly pieces with a lustrous surface. Objects such as bright metal buttons or bottle caps can also be included to create sparkling, free-form compositions.

Mosaic is indispensable for disguising unsightly features or brightening up colourless ones. Ugly expanses of concrete, plastic rain barrels and urns, garden sheds and outbuildings can all have new life breathed into them as decorative artworks. Eating alfresco can be transformed by adding mosaic to garden furniture. A table-top is relatively straightforward to decorate and mosaic forms a level, hard-wearing surface; chairs, benches and stools take a little more time but look just as good.

right Mosaic forms a solid and durable surface for garden furniture. Here the use of bold, geometric blocks of colour makes a focal point of this table.

centre Designed by Kate Otten, this serpent, set directly into the floor, is a delightful way to draw the eye towards the interior.

far right Using shards of crockery set into cement, this wall decoration at Maison Picassiette, Chartres, is by the folk artist Raymond Isidore.

Children are naturally drawn to the bright palette of mosaic and to the technique, which has much in common with collage and where you can see your results almost instantly. Mosaic can be used to make all sorts of appealing pieces: boxes for toys, borders for play areas, pictures set into walls and chequered grids for outdoor games such as snakes and ladders, draughts or ludo. The grids, if carefully planned, can double up as areas of decorative paving set into grass or an existing path. The technique is simple, and you can involve the younger members of the family in the design and construction, creating a section at a time.

The sheer brilliance of mosaic is magnified by water, whether it be spring rain or a trickling brook. Mosaic continues to be a popular material for lining pools of any size. Placing mosaic near a fountain or water source or, even better, constructing a shallow pool of iridescent mosaic, will give any garden a focal point. The mosaic will naturally change the appearance of the water, so deep blues will give a Mediterranean feel, while green will evoke fresh water. You can have great fun with designs, creating *trompe l'oeil* effects with crabs, lobsters, fish or water plants on the bottom of the pool, or opt for a more classical pattern with a plain mosaic and a geometric border. Around the edge of the pool a simple pattern of colourful mixed mosaic or a series of repeat motifs is equally effective.

Mosaic is also ideal for decorating fountains. A cheap manufactured fountain can be changed beyond all recognition with a coating of water-repellent cement and a selection of colourful tesserae. If you have a water pump you can create your own small fountain with a good-sized metal funnel. Add mosaic tiles to the exterior of the funnel, place it over the pump and you have an instant fountain. You can also mosaic around a water spout built into a wall to make anything from a classical Roman head to a mythical creature.

mosaic practicalities

Basic mosaic materials are tesserae, either ceramic or glass (smalti), which are available pre-cut, from specialist outlets or by mail order, in a rich spectrum of colours. Marble and stone can also be used but will often require professional cutting. Mosaic is the perfect way to recycle beads, buttons, broken crockery, glass, mirrors and tiles. Broken tiles can often be obtained for a token fee from tile shops, and much recyled material can be collected from boot sales, skips and from friends. A wide range of found objects from plastic toys to glass marbles can also be incorporated in mosaic work.

Tools needed for mosaic-making are either spring-loaded nippers, which will cut both glass and ceramic, or a glass-cutter and a tile-cutter, a Stanley knife, a palette knife, pliers and, for grouting and cementing, a sponge and trowel.

Mosaic will adhere to plastic, wood, ceramic, metal, concrete and many other materials. A cement or adhesive is needed for fixing the mosaic tiles to the surface, and then a grout is used to fill the gaps between tiles and make a smooth, durable finish. Different approaches are required for different surfaces. All exterior mosaic work needs water- and frost-resistant cement and grout. For plastic and metal use an exterior tile adhesive. Wood needs to be sealed first with a diluted solution of PVA (polyvinyl acetate) adhesive. For ceramics and concrete use an exterior cement-based adhesive. The grout can be coloured with acrylic paint or cement dye to create different effects and make areas of the design stand out. Always wear goggles when cutting mosaic pieces, and rubber gloves for cementing and grouting.

Small-scale mosaics are a good way for the beginner to experiment with techniques and the effects of different patterns.

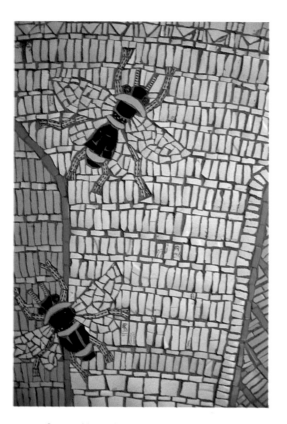

above This work by Cleo Mussi is made entirely of recycled glazed crockery which has been painstakingly cut into 2cm (¾in) strips. Although the bees' wings are a similar colour to the background, positioning the tiles at a different angle ensures they stand out. Decorative shards have been carefully chosen to make the legs.

right Marble and plain and decorated ceramic tiles set into cement make up this decorative pool-side design. The three-dimensional effect of the central motif is achieved by using contrasting dark and light marbles. The background of irregular paving is a pleasing foil to the formal star, and is easy to create as no cutting is required.

above left Stylized ceramic roses, made of shards of china set into cement that has been painted with leaves and stems, show how mundane materials can be turned into exquisite compositions.

above right This detail shows the close relationship of mosaic to patchwork. Made of recycled Victorian china, highly glazed, printed and plain, this piece is evocative of times past. The materials, including a fragment of script and a faded photographic image, contribute to this effect, and the lustrous gold grout in which the shards are embedded gives the piece a jewel-like quality.

left A detail of a dragon sculpture in a children's playground in Japan, this section is made up of lustre-glazed ceramic formed into discs that cleverly imitate the scales of the dragon in their shape and slightly reptilian texture.

'The quirkiest assemblages are clad in a jigsaw of ceramic history recycled to form the personalities of my characters.'

Cleo Mussi

CleoMussi

mosaic figures

Cleo Mussi's initial training in textiles has had a major influence on her mosaic work. She treats undecorated surfaces in much the same way as she would a plain fabric, combining colour, texture and pattern to create a vibrant surface design. Elements of embroidery, weaving and lace-making are also visible in her mosaic patterns. Since Mussi uses a lot of salvaged material she is naturally drawn to cultures that have a history of recycling, such as India and Africa. She also finds inspiration in traditional Islamic and Moroccan rugs and Yemeni architecture, with its brightly painted detail.

Mussi's compositions feature shards of ceramic, glass, slate and *objets trouvés* such as old crockery lids, spouts and handles. She can transform the most unglamorous and unlikely utilitarian objects into artworks – old saucepans and frying pans become decorative wall pieces, for example, while funnels, tin bowls and biscuit tins form the physiognomy of her totem-like mosaic figures.

The figures here are made from garden tools. Mussi makes preliminary sketches for her mosaic design in crayon, but ultimately the composition is dictated by the selection of materials. Before starting to make a mosaic figure it is worth spending time hunting for old plates and tiles to break up for the mosaic pieces.

Cleo Mussi's charming cast of mosaic characters have cup handles for ears and trowels and funnels for heads and bodies. The different shaped mosaic pieces are arranged to suggest facial features such as nose or eyebrows.

materials and equipment

Broken crockery or tiles for the mosaic shards, nippers, plastic funnel, sharp knife, garden trowel, wood glue, paint brush, scrim (fabric tape), spatula, exterior tile adhesive, rubber gloves, grey floor-tile grout, black cement dye, dust mask, cloth, toothbrush.

1 Your mosaic pieces can be taken from broken crockery or tiles, in a variety of colours, patterns and finishes, which will create stunning visual effects on the completed item. Use nippers (available at mosaic or tile shops) to break the crockery into small shards.

2 Make the basic shape of your spade figure. Cut off the end of a plastic funnel with a sharp knife and insert an upside-down trowel into the hole. Paint the trowel handle and the funnel with wood glue, then wrap around the scrim as you would a bandage.

3 Using a spatula, spread a layer of exterior tile adhesive on to the skirt surface. Then, starting with the flower patterns on the skirt, stick on the mosaic pieces, working from the centre of each flower out and filling in the gaps in-between afterwards.

4 For the face of the figure, cover the trowel head with exterior tile adhesive and scrim, then pick out the facial features with coloured pieces of mosaic, creating the eyes, cheeks, nose and lips.

5 Next, grout the figure. You can use grey floor-tile grout for this or ready-made grout in white. In both cases you can add black cement dye to the grout to create a more interesting effect, giving the composition more definition. For the best results, smooth on the grout by hand, but wear rubber gloves for this task.

6 Rub off the excess with a cloth or a small scrubbing brush (a toothbrush is excellent for this). Wear gloves and a dust mask while you are doing this. Leave overnight for the grout to dry.

siting and fixing

Cleo Mussi's figure is suited to numerous garden positions. This free-standing piece looks equally at home against a background of greenery or distressed wood, in the vegetable patch or the herbaceous border. A group of mosaic figures makes a quirky feature. The joy of this work is that it can be moved to different parts of the garden, depending on the season. Always place it in a sheltered area as winds may cause damage, and take it inside for the winter.

'Mosaic is a language of endless possibilities and translations'

Rebecca Newnham

Rebecca**Newnham**

mosaic disc

Rebecca Newnham has the Midas touch, turning mundane works into glittering prizes. After studying glass and ceramics, she changed direction to mosaic. The extraordinary organic shapes formed by blown glass have influenced her work, as has Byzantine mosaic. She adopted the technique of Byzantine artists of angling tesserae to increase their reflective qualities, applying them to curved surfaces to further enhance the effect. In addition she has developed a base using Styrofoam, a dense form of polystyrene, which, unlike traditional mosaic bases, can be carved and is far better suited to her fluid, sinuous compositions.

Newnham selects her materials from the iridescent end of the mosaic spectrum in glitter-ball hues. She currently works almost exclusively with glass tesserae, which she paints with coloured enamels, gold leaf, aluminium and silver. She creates her work in stages: a preliminary sketch is followed by a painting which introduces colour and often texture in the form of collage; finally she lays the mosaic on to the base.

The mirror mosaic disc shown here consists of mirror tiles laid on a fibreglass base. Both the base and the mosaic are relatively straightforward to make, though you need to allow a day or two for the base to dry before starting on the mosaic. Unless you are experienced in glass-cutting, it is best to buy ready-cut mirror tiles.

This glittering mirror mosaic disc can be displayed as it is or half-filled with water, which will serve to heighten its reflective qualities.

materials and equipment

Large plate or dish, wax parting agent, 15 x 46cm (6 x 18in) fibreglass strips, rubber gloves, epoxy resin, brush, pencil, hacksaw, surform (file with a curved edge), ready-cut mirror tiles or mirror glass, circular-cutter (optional), glass-cutter, palette knife, non-porous tile adhesive, fine grout, dry soft cloth.

1 Use a large plate or dish to make your mould, and cover its base with a wax parting agent – this will allow you to remove the dish once the shape has set. Protecting your hands with rubber gloves, lay strips of fibreglass on to the wax parting agent.

2 Brush on a layer of epoxy resin. This will wet the fibreglass and make it set rigid. When the first layer of fibreglass is dry (it will take about a day), add another layer and brush on more resin. You will need at least two layers in total.

3 Leave until touch dry, mark out the edge of the dish with a pencil, then slip the dish out of the mould. Saw around the pencil line with a hacksaw. Using a file with a curved edge, smooth any rough edges and bumps from the dish.

4 For the central piece of the mosaic use a circle of mirror or, if you prefer, a triangular shape, or a pebble or button. If you are an experienced glass-cutter, cut the circle yourself using a circular-cutter. Otherwise a glazier should be able to do it.

5 Square mirror tiles can be easily bought. If you want to make your own mirror tiles you will need a sheet of mirror approximately 1m sq (3ft sq). Mark up and score with a glass-cutter 2.5cm (1in) strips vertically and horizontally. Snap the strips by hand. You will need a total of about 800 pieces for both inner and outer surfaces.

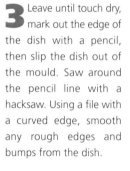

6 With a palette knife, smooth a 3mm (⅛in) layer of non-porous tile adhesive over an area in the middle of the dish. Place the circular mosaic piece in the centre, then lay the small squares around it, working towards the outer edge of the dish in widening circles.

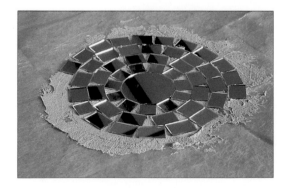

7 Smooth on more adhesive as you work, but avoid putting on too much at once as it will dry out if left exposed. When you have tiled the inside of the dish, turn it over and tile the outside.

8 Once you have finished tiling the dish, cover the mosaic in a layer of grout. Use a fine mix to avoid scratching the glass. Scoop it on and smooth it over the surface with a gloved hand. While it is still wet (between 10 minutes and 2 hours depending on the weather) rub off as much as possible with a dry cloth.

siting and fixing

Rebecca Newnham's shimmering mosaic disc, with its subtle palette and strong reflective qualities, should be placed where light will play off its brilliant surface, preferably dappled sunlight. This free-standing piece needs no special fixing and would look good fringed by soft feathery grasses or plants such as poppies, whose brilliant colours will be reflected in its surface. As long as you have used weather-proof tile adhesive and grout, the disc can stay outside all year.

Slate, with its satin sheen, pebbles, with their smooth rounded contours, and shells, with their delicate and varied forms, are perfect natural materials for garden ornament. Together they are capable of magical feats, adding texture, colour and focus to unremarkable or problem areas of the garden and transforming utilitarian items into works of art. At their best after rain when they glisten with vibrancy, slate, pebbles and shells have been used for centuries to create works that are both durable and decorative.

slate, pebble & shell

left Pebbles are at their glistening best when wet. Contemporary makers often exploit this quality, incorporating them in water features. **above** Graded ovoid pebbles are juxtaposed with slivers of slate to delineate a swallow on the wing.

a history of slate

Slate is formed over millions of years from the sediment and mud at the bottom of ancient seas, which have dried, hardened and compressed. Occurring naturally in fine layers, it can be used either as a solid block or split into paper-thin slivers. Slate is found mainly in Europe and America.

Used for roofs since Roman times, slate was also for centuries the material of blackboards, and, of course, school slates. Medieval roofers working on the great cathedrals of Europe exploited slate's decorative potential, laying slates alternately with or against the grain to create diverse patterns.

The north Wales slate industry began in the mid-eighteenth century, reaching a peak during the nineteenth century when Welsh quarries were the largest slate producers in the world. Until the end of the eighteenth century, slate-quarrying methods were crude and output was limited, but with the industrial revolution new methods of production were introduced to meet the huge demand for slate for roofs, steps, floors, mantelpieces, hearths and lintels for new building programmes. Slate also found wide popularity in gardens as a material for crazy paving. In areas where slate was quarried, slabs were used as fencing.

Welsh slate was exported to early American colonies. America's first slate quarry, in Pennsylvania, did not open until 1785 but by the end of the nineteenth century there were over 200 there. As a consequence of this increased availability internationally, slate began to attract the attention of artists and craftspeople. During the nineteenth century it became popular as a medium for a variety of objects ranging from tables to fans made of the finest sections of slate, demonstrating both the delicacy of the material and its sturdiness.

The introduction of cheaper alternatives to slate during the twentieth century led to its decline as a roofing material. However, at the same time interest has rapidly increased in the potential for making environmental sculpture and garden ornament out of both newly quarried and recycled slate.

a history of pebble and shell

Shells were one of the earliest forms of decoration, and have been used for thousands of years, particularly by those living closest to the natural supply – along the sea-shore. Pierced shells, threaded and worn as ornamentation, have been found in prehistoric sites in central France and were used during the Stone Age in a rudimentary way as tools and vessels. The shell has also been valued as

far left With age, slate often acquires lichens and mosses on its surface, and its grey-blue colouring becomes more intense.

centre Sumptuous wall and floor decoration at the sixteenth-century Nymphaeum at Lainate near Milan is rendered in Ligurian black limestone and quartz.

left This simple geometric design on the island of Tilos is typical of Greek pebble-mosaic work passed down the centuries.

currency by many cultures through history, from the wampum (shell necklaces) of the American Indians to the cowrie shells of African tribespeople.

Pebble-work decoration using smooth, sea-worn pebbles has been used for many centuries. The earliest known example is an eighth century BC pebble-mosaic floor at Gordium, Asia Minor. In ancient Greece it was used extensively to make durable cobbled pathways with figurative and geometrical designs. *Coclackia*, the Greek name for pebble work, is onomatopoeic, imitating the sound of feet on cobblestones. In China pebble mosaic has been a traditional element of garden design for over 2,000 years, and at Suzhou, the 'Garden City', bold, geometric pebble designs can still be seen.

Pebbles and shells unleashed the artistic imagination of the Romans. They embraced them lavishly, capitalizing on their associations with cool breezes and clear water, often combining them to embellish grottoes, caves and shady alcoves and as a contrast to their classical garden schemes.

In Britain cobblestones were a standard paving material for centuries, especially in the north of England. Although most were used to form plain, functional surfaces, evidence of naive figurative compositions can still be seen in towns such as Lytham St Anne's in Lancashire.

During the late sixteenth and seventeenth centuries a new fashion in garden design, which originated in Rome, swept north through Europe, first to Florence, then France and later to England. Grottoes – artificially constructed or naturally occurring cave-like places – were covered from floor to ceiling with dense designs in pebbles and shells, painstakingly selected and graded to form perfect patterns. These decorations were often coated in green wax, to emulate moss and further increase the subterranean atmosphere, while pools and dripping water added to the gloom.

The walls and floors of the Nymphaeum at Lainate near Milan, begun in 1580, are covered with elaborate patterns using black and white pebbles with such artistry that the effect is of textured wallpaper. The first grotto constructed in England at Woburn Abbey, Bedfordshire in about 1627 resulted in the building of literally hundreds of other grottoes around the country, all based on Italian Renaissance designs. At Versailles the Grotto de Thétis was completed in 1664. At Rozendaal near Arnhem in the Netherlands, a shell gallery added in the seventeenth century consists of a series of alcoves each encrusted with shell decoration over which water drips constantly to keep the colours vivid and the tone sombre.

The extraordinary gardens of Isola Bella, on an island in Lake Maggiore, Italy, were also built in the mid-seventeenth century in the shape of an immense galleon. They boasted not only a grotto but also numerous other features all incorporating intricate pebble work. The builders took advantage of readily available local materials, using pebbles from the lake to create alcoves and form a decorative surface for paths.

While early grottoes were subdued in their use of materials, as the seventeenth century progressed a palette of shells, pebbles and rocks was supplemented by ammonites, spar and quartz, semi-precious stones, coral and tufa (pitted limestone, relished for its water-worn appearance) in increasingly elaborate compositions. Walls and ceilings glistened with geological riches, while pebbles worked in elaborate patterns were a popular choice for floor designs. The decoration of these follies was often left to the ladies of the house and, since they were relatively wealthy, they were able to supplement native materials with exotic shells brought from as far away as the East and West Indies and West Africa.

The fashion for grottoes eventually waned, but the use of these materials in a garden setting had been firmly established. Their legacy can be seen in Victorian rock gardens and ferneries and, most spectacularly, in the work of two cousins, Jane and Mary Parminter, who settled in Devon after ten years on a Grand Tour of Europe and built a hexagonal house decorated to their own taste. The result is an extravagant, shell-encrusted marvel,

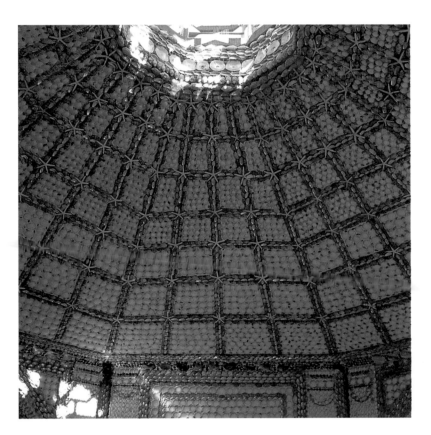

far left A grotto floor at Pistoia in Italy uses a combination of marble strips, shards and dark pebbles to create a dramatic composition which has rhythm and texture.

left This geometric grotto ceiling incorporates starfish as well as shells in its regular design.

where walls, ceilings and staircases are covered with shell designs combined with feathers, bone, sand, lichen and broken china.

Shell collecting first developed as a pastime in the eighteenth century, and by Victorian times it was such a popular activity that entire auctions were devoted to the sale of shells. Inspired by health-giving trips to the seaside, enthusiasts in America and Britain took up shell work as a hobby, using shells to cover anything from boxes and frames to walls and small buildings. Shell work was a particular feature of the seaside villa.

Today examples of modern and historical pebble work, made using traditional materials and designs, can still be seen in Greece, particularly on the island of Lindos. Contemporary works can also be found in parts of Spain, Portugal and Latin America which all have a long tradition of pebble work. It is increasingly used to create hard-wearing, decorative surfaces in public and private spaces, with designs ranging from the classical and figurative to the abstract. Shell work is also as popular as ever, and in the hands of contemporary makers its applications are even wider and more varied.

slate in the garden

Much more than simply grey, slate comes in a brilliant range of deep hues. Each slate-mining region produces its own subtle shades, including smoky blues, greens and pinks. For example, Welsh slate ranges from the blue-grey of Ffestiniog to the reddish-purple of Caernarfonshire, while Pennsylvania slate is a deep blue-black, and slate from Virginia is particularly lustrous due to its high mica content. Slate can also be coloured by treatments at quarries with subtle pastel shades, adding to its beauty and versatility. Water has a transforming effect on slate, bringing out its deeper colours, so it is often at its most vivid by a fountain or gushing stream, or after a shower of rain. Currently hot property with interior designers and landscape architects alike, who see the potential of this natural, durable material, it is now being used for everything from conservatory flooring and work surfaces to garden urns and paving.

Paving by laying slates horizontally is the easiest and most popular use of slate. Different patterns and textures can be created by cutting the slate into diamonds or squares and by laying alternate tiles at right angles. For a more dramatic and unusual effect, requiring considerably more work to achieve, you can lay a path by sinking slates vertically into the ground for a delicious, rough, striated finish with a texture reminiscent of *mille-feuille* pastry.

Like most hard surfaces, a slate path needs to be softened by planting, and it is the perfect foil for delicate foliage. Imagine a blue-grey slate path edged by mounds of lavender after a summer shower, or a reddish-purple slate path winding through a bed of *Trillium sessile* in the spring.

Slate also makes a good edging material, either to delineate the edge of a lawn, or to create a feature in itself. In the herb garden, for example, slate can be used both as a border around the garden and to divide the plot into different sections.

right A contemporary use of slate is illustrated in this Scottish bridge made by Joe Smith who takes advantage of slate's colour and texture to create contrasting architectural detailing.

far left Photographed after rain, when slate is at its most vibrant, a serpentine wall topped with slate is surrounded with plants in complementary shades of purple and silver.

left Large slate standing stones are used as an edging in this shady, fern-filled area of the garden.

It will give a sense of formality and structure with its crisp lines, deepen in colour when it rains and will provide an added dimension to the planting once the flowering has finished. In winter, the skeleton of the herb garden will form a bare, geometric pattern. Slate's rich and varying colours form the perfect backdrop for a large variety of herbs from purple sage (*Salvia officinalis* 'Purpurascens') to the button-like yellow flowers of tansy (*Tanacetum vulgare*) to the flamboyant purple pompons of *Allium giganteum*.

Combined with pebbles and shells, slate becomes more versatile – its smooth, dark sheen and its consistency make it ideal for sharp detail and for motifs more difficult to delineate in other materials. Slate also makes a very effective traditional Welsh fence – upright slabs are set in the ground and joined with wire.

Contemporary makers are finding ever more innovative uses for slate, particularly for making monumental, sculptural shapes. These forms can be made using a technique similar to dry-stone walling. The slates' craggy appearance and rich colours make you see the material with fresh eyes.

slate practicalities

Slate is mainly available in the areas it is mined and can be bought directly from quarries, either in large pieces or as assorted offcuts known as quarry dressing. You can ask the quarry to cut and dress the slate for you but this will bump up the price substantially. Alternatively, there are often years of use left in redundant roof tiles.

Tools required for working with slate are minimal – a thin, broad-edged chisel, a lump hammer, a slate knife and a hard metal edge. The

two main techniques are splitting (cutting slate from a larger piece into smaller sections with a broad-edged chisel and a lump hammer) and dressing (shaping the slate with a hammer and chisel or slate knife over a hard metal edge). Both require skill and practice to perfect. Always wear goggles when cutting and dressing slate.

Beginners should start by making a small paved area with fairly thin slivers of slate before graduating to three-dimensional works. To get a feel for working with slate in three dimensions, start by building a small, abstract free-standing piece. As with dry-stone walling, slate works can be constructed without using cement to bond the individual slates together. If the slates are placed carefully, their weight will settle to form a solid, durable mass. Keep checking the stability of the slates as you build up the piece.

pebbles in the garden

Pebble work is a versatile, long-lasting medium that can be adapted to suit any garden style, providing a welcome alternative to more mundane paving materials. It has a subdued natural palette from coal black to the palest yellow, making it easy on the eye and in harmony with the environment. Once in place, pebble work forms an enduring surface, like a rough-weave carpet. By virtue of its weight it tends to be confined to pathways or parterres, but small, light pebbles can also be incorporated into walls and ceilings. From a practical point of view pebble work also keeps interiors cool.

Its designs are enlivened by strong textural qualities and fluid lines. Essentially classical in character, pebble work has a natural affinity with formal garden schemes, but abstract or geometrical designs, especially when limited to two contrasting shades, make a dramatic impact in the spare design of modern gardens.

Pebble work needs to be used with care, especially in confined spaces: its texture, colour and form make it a focal point. Before deciding on any design, think about the nearby plants. The rough texture of pebbles makes a pleasing contrast with plants with feathery foliage such as lady's mantle (*Alchemilla mollis*), with its soft, velvety leaves and fine sprays of greenish-yellow flowers, or the ornamental grass (*Pennisetum villosum*), which has pale fluffy bristles. Alternatively, for real drama try architectural plants such as the evergreen sea holly (*Eryngium proteiflorum*), with spiky, silvery bracts and dark, cone-shaped flower heads, *Eucomis comosa*, with its boldly spotted stems, shiny leaves and yellowy-green ornamental flowers, or the brilliant pink pompons of *Allium rosenbachianum*.

For a small garden, a perfect design would be a spiral that draws the eye towards a favourite garden work at the centre, such as an urn or sundial. Another way to introduce pebble work in a smaller garden is to confine it to one area, perhaps by concentrating on steps or using it as a border to a path or paved area.

Pebble work can be personalized – for example, by making a series of small pebble-work squares to record the birth of children, or family anniversaries, which could be added to over the years. For a slightly whimsical effect, try a pebble-work mat for

right Nothing could be simpler than this pebble-work design beneath birch trees. Circular and radiating lines create a sense of space and well-being.

far right A feature of this unusual Japanese wall inset with pebbles is the tall column at its centre topped with a large glass orb.

left Groups of pebbles, chosen for their autumnal cream and rust tones, top these metal rods to make a tall, spiky fence.

outside the front door or, in the summerhouse, a Persian pebble rug complete with fringes for the floor and brilliant pebble murals for the walls.

In gardens where space is not an issue you can go to town, covering whole courtyards or terraces or creating a serpentine path that leads the eye towards the horizon, linking different areas of the garden. If the floors of porches, other entrances and conservatories are treated in the same way, it will give a unity to house and garden.

Pebble work is an ideal edging for ponds and pools, especially where it will receive a regular drenching. The uneven surfaces have a practical use in alerting those with impaired vision to a potential hazard. Pebbles are equally successful in a water channel and around a fountain or spout. Pebbles can also be used to create sculptural forms, such as cairn-like structures. If drilled they can be threaded on to metal posts to form a modern-looking barrier.

pebble practicalities

Pebble work is a craft that requires heavy manual labour. Whereas small pieces can be built in situ, larger works are easiest made in sections and reassembled on site. Pebbles should be collected in moderation and with permission – beaches and river beds are both good sources. Never collect pebbles from conservation areas. You can also buy pebbles at some DIY stores.

To make pebble work you need a trowel, a shovel (for mixing concrete for setting your composition), a tamping bar and a kneeler – it's hard on the knees. Beginners should start with a small, abstract piece using a simple design that concentrates on texture and rhythm.

Before starting work, make a sketch of the design and decide which type of stone is to be used where. To make a good foundation for a pebble floor, prepare the ground by digging out and levelling. Place a good curbing of stone around the edges to keep the composition symmetrical. Lay the pebbles on a bed of dry sand, grit and cement, arranging them until you are happy with the effect, then tamp them down and apply a grout of sieved, dry sand and cement with a fine brush. Once the design is finished, wet the mix with a fine spray and leave it to set. Add a top layer of grout to ensure the work is fixed solidly.

127

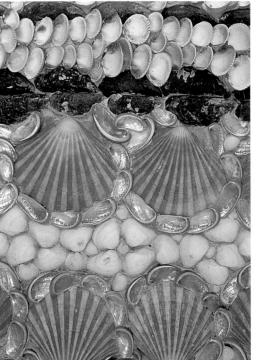

far left The design of this circular paving by Marc Schoellen has a mystic quality. Fossil shells radiate out from a glittering crystal ball laid on gold leaf.

left A detail of the interior of the Shell House at Ballymaloe, Ireland has a sumptuous central motif of scallop shells trimmed with a glittering edging of abalone.

shells in the garden

Light, delicate and often vividly coloured, shells can be used to create the most detailed decoration. Capable of effecting complete transformations, they are an excellent way to renovate the old and brighten up the dull, from terracotta pots and plastic planters to entire rooms. Unlike most pebbles, shells are lightweight enough to be used safely to form patterns on a ceiling.

Shells have the advantage of being easy and quick to apply – it only takes a few hours to revamp small objects such as window-boxes, turning them into mini works of art that will last for years. A simple but attractive design for a shell pot can be made using scallop shells as a central motif set against a background of smaller shells of a contrasting colour. Filled with ferns, hostas or other shade-loving plants and placed in dark spot, it can bring an overlooked or difficult area of the garden to life. Shells look particularly beautiful when decorating planters placed close to or actually in water – their natural environment.

Where immature planting leaves areas of bare wall, shells can be used to create inexpensive and effective murals. If you want your shell compositions to have a lower profile, use small repeat motifs, such as circles, squares, diamonds or crosses placed at regular intervals, rather than covering a whole expanse of wall.

While the design of your garden may dictate restraint, in a garden room you can unleash your decorative fantasies, fabricating your own personal folly. Wooden or brick -structures, from summerhouses to garden porches, old or new, make ideal subjects for transformation. You can work on any scale you like, covering a wall, floor, ceiling, table-top, stool or even a picture frame with designs in shells of all colours, shapes and sizes.

shell practicalities

To preserve beaches from erosion, avoid collecting shells yourself – in general, use only shells left over from a seafood restaurant or your own cooking, such as scallops and mussels, oysters and cockles. You can also buy shells from specialist suppliers. Alternatively, try hunting at second-hand shops and boot sales for old shell necklaces and boxes that can be dismantled and the raw materials reused.

Tools needed for shell work include pliers and a palette knife. Before starting work, wash and dry your shells and grade them into sizes, types and colours. Better results are usually obtained if you allow the materials themselves to suggest the design, rather than the other way round.

You can either make up the design on a piece of chipboard or plywood to be set in cement later or work directly on to the cement. If you are placing shells concave side down in the design you may need to fill the interior of each shell with an all-purpose filler to create a solid surface which will adhere more strongly. For small objects use tile grout to fix the shells. For exterior use or for the interiors of garden buildings, shell work should be laid in cement. Projects for beginners include containers or small shell panels, which will allow experimentation with different effects.

left Emma Stabler's shell design for this planter makes the most of different shell shapes. The razor shells look particularly appropriate for the strong linear decoration

GALLERY water features

above A highly contemporary landscape water feature uses polished metal topped with shells. The undulating quality of the work is an intentional reference to the sea, while playful jets of water ensure the shells retain their vivid colours.

right A formal garden feature by George Carter makes equal reference to grottoes and the elegant garden ornament of the eighteenth century. Composed of many different materials, this is a delightful study in textures. The lead urn effect is achieved using glazed ceramic, while the background is a rich carpet of mussel shells.

centre This monumental fountain at Kew Gardens in London is composed of spirals of thin pieces of slate, emphasizing its delicacy. The strong horizontal lines of the work are offset by the gently cascading water.

left Features such as this stone cairn are becoming increasingly popular, showing the influence of environmental artists such as Andy Goldsworthy. Here the natural beauty and irregular sizes of the pebbles have been emphasized by juxtaposing different shapes and colours, creating a natural, beautiful composition.

below left This formal pebble-work composition by Julie Toll has a strong grid of curved and straight lines defined by stone edges. The random pebble-work paving links different areas, while the rich colours of the pebbles in the central rill draw the eye in towards the gravel beds planted with alpines.

below Seemingly random, this composition contrasts rounded pebbles against long, spiky shards of slate. The pebble-lined pool is fed by a trickling pipe.

'Pebbles are a fascinating material, each a small miracle produced by natural forces'

Maggy Howarth

Maggy**Howarth**

pebble sun ray

Maggy Howarth has turned the ancient art of pebble work into a contemporary art form. Her work in public squares and private gardens is a legacy that will endure for centuries. Howarth originally trained as a painter and moved into theatre design. A keen gardener, it was while designing her own large farmhouse garden that she became interested in garden features and surface design. She made her first pebble work for her own garden.

Her ideas come from diverse sources – the materials themselves, the location in which the work will be placed and her background in the theatre. Classical Greek and Roman pebble mosaic, the abstract qualities of Islamic tile patterns and Portuguese pavements all have an influence.

Howarth's technique is simple but painstaking. She walks for hours collecting her materials and then grades her harvest by colour and size. The simple geometric design of the fan-shaped paved area illustrated opposite plays with texture, colour and scale, showing just how effective a simple pattern can be. In this muscular composition pebbles of graduating size have been chosen, using texture and form to dramatic effect. It illustrates perfectly Howarth's point that a good design 'must be bold, has to have a contrast and needs to be deliberate but not fussy'.

The radiating lines of Maggy Howarth's pebble sun ray are designed to draw the eye towards the seat beyond. Pictured here before its final application of sand and cement, the surface will be durable and practical.

materials and equipment

Spade, broken stone or brick, gritty gravel mix, sledgehammer, tamper, spirit level, grit, fine and builders' sand, fresh cement, long block of wood, trowel, pebbles, plastic boxes, stout rubber gloves, plastic cover for wet weather, brush.

1 Prepare the site. Dig out the topsoil and fill to within about 10cm (4in) of ground level with bits of broken stone or brick to form the hardcore base (the top of the final pebble design will be just above the level of the surrounding ground). Pour on a layer of gritty gravel.

dry-mix concrete

a 3 parts grit
b 2 parts mixture of fine and builders' sand
c 1 part fresh cement

2 Compact the surface with a sledgehammer so that the gritty gravel mixture fills in all the holes between the stone and brick. Continue to tamp down with a tamper, and use a spirit level to check that the surface is even, allowing a slight run-off for rain water.

3 Add a layer of dry-mix concrete which will set under normal atmospheric conditions. Ensure you carry out the project from this part until completion in fine weather, otherwise the dry-mix conrete will get wet, messy, and start to harden. Mark out your pattern, using pieces of wood and a trowel to score straight lines. Sort the pebbles into boxes or piles according to size and colour.

4 Lay the pebbles by pushing them firmly into the dry-mix concrete. Bed them in vertically with the smallest side facing upwards – this will ensure they will not come loose at a later stage. Check they are packed tightly together. If you are doing a large area or geometric design, it may be helpful to subdivide the design or do all recurring patterns together to ensure they are regularly spaced.

5 Between the lines of pale pebbles, lay two rows of darker ones. Angle the rows of dark pebbles down and towards each other to create a slight herringbone pattern. Once the pebbles have been laid, tap them down firmly with a block of wood to make the surface even. Adjust as necessary.

6 When you have finished, spray with water to start the hardening process and settle the mix between the pebbles. Leave overnight then use another mix of three parts fine dry sand to one part fresh cement, brushing it over the surface. Work the mixture down well into all the joints to within 1cm (½in) of the tops of the pebbles. This will seal the surface. Use a fine spray to clean the pebbles.

siting and fixing

After laying the pebbles and spraying them with water, leave the area covered with polythene for a week so that the sand and cement mix will harden and cure. Then the surface will be ready to walk on, and should withstand years of use. Brush it with a stiff brush to remove leaves and other garden debris. This pebble area makes an eye-catching feature embedded among flagstones. You can also surround it with creeping ground-cover plants if you want to soften the edges so that it blends into the garden.

'I make simple forms that allow the materials to express themselves – the materials are my inspiration'

Joe Smith

JoeSmith

slate urn

The stone mason Joe Smith was brought up in the wild, windswept scenery of the West Yorkshire Pennines, a landscape he has since exchanged for the equally wild west coast of Scotland. For him the landscape and its natural materials are a source of enduring fascination and inspiration.

He learned the art of dry-stone walling from an old shepherd. As he says, 'You couldn't live in the high dales without being aware of dry-stone walling'. Such was his passion for stone that he used to go out and build walls for pleasure whenever he had a spare moment. His reputation as a fine craftsman began to develop as a result. Today Smith works with any sort of stone from granite to lakeland stone, producing work for outdoor settings ranging from walls and pillars to bridges and cascades.

Smith's work with slate uses the same technique as dry-stone walling. He often uses reclaimed slate, relishing the marks made by the original craftsman and rising to the challenge of finding another use for it. His slate urn, pictured opposite, needs no cement to hold it in position. Each slate, carefully selected and cut, interlocks with another to form a monumental garden feature combining both natural beauty and formal splendour. For the best results, practise cutting slate until you are quite proficient, and take time as you build the urn to keep the outline neat and strong.

The rough, textured surface of Joe Smith's slate urn is in playful contrast to its refined, classical form.

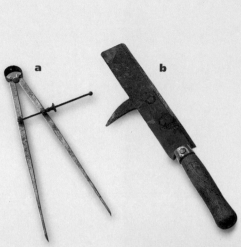

1 Choose the site – you need to make the urn in situ as it will be impossible to move once built. Clear an area the size that the urn will be at its widest and spread concrete over it, smoothing and levelling as you go. Cover the concrete with a flagstone – the older the better, and ideally with a little moss growing over it. Use a spirit level to check that the surface is level.

materials and equipment

Concrete, flagstone, spirit level, about 250kg (¼ ton) slate, dividers **a**, slate knife **b**, metal beam, hammer, fine wide chisel, drill with masonry bit.

2 Mark out a circle about 30cm (12in) in diameter on a piece of slate. Place the slate over a hard edge, and use a slate knife to cut out the shape, rotating the slate as you go. Lay the circle in the centre of the flagstone to make the first layer. Start layering pieces of slate on top of the circle.

3 A metal beam makes a good anvil for cutting the slate with the slate knife. Bring the knife straight down on to the slate to make as clean a cut as possible.

4 Build up the layers of slate, in gradually widening circles, to form the shape of the urn. The final height will be about 60cm (2ft). Keep checking that the outline is still symmetrical, and go back and adjust as necessary.

5 To split the slate into smaller pieces, use a hammer and a fine wide chisel. Keep tapping the chisel along your chosen split line, listening until you hear the slate start to open up. This process is called riving. Hold the slate upright between your feet to keep it steady. Wear stout boots or walking boots, in case the chisel slips.

6 Finally, make two rings to finish off the top of the urn. Cut two circles of slate then mark out an inner circle at the centre of each with dividers. Drill about 20 holes around each inner circle. Carefully hammer out the centre using a ball-peen hammer. Bond a little cement or mastic beneath the circles to fix them in place if the urn is in a very windy location.

siting and fixing

A vase of this size sits well in a formal situation, such as at the centre of a parterre, where its symmetrical lines are emphasized. Alternatively, if it is placed on a weathered wall its rugged solidity will be apparent. Delicate and feathery foliage will form a pleasing contrast with the urn's dense form.

suppliers addresses and websites

metal

Atlas Metal Sales
1401 Umatilla Street
Denver, CO 80204
TEL: 1-800-662-0143
www.atlasmetal.com
Art Sculpture Specialty Metals
Wherehouse (Aluminum Ingot,
Pewter, Bronze, Cooper Sheet
& Coil)

Bonny Doon Engineering
TEL: 1-800-335-9962
www.bonnydoonengineering.com
Metal & Metal Smithing Tools

glass

Bullseye Glass Company
The Bullseye Connection
Resource Center
1308 NW Everett
Portland, OR 97209
TEL: 503-227-2797
www.bullseye-glass.com
Stained Glass & Glass Gift Ware

Khue.com
3703 Spring Street

Eureka, CA 95503
TEL: 707-442-4203
www.khue.com
Stained Glass Supplies Online
(Glass, Cutters, Soldiering Supplies)

Stained Glass Web Mart
www.glassmart.com
TEL: 1-888-GLASS-96 (Orders Only)
Stained Glass, Grinders, Copper Foil,
Chemicals

ceramics

Busy Bee Ceramics
P.O. Box 2642
St. Louis, MI 63116
TEL: 314-481-3884
www.busybeeceramics.com
Stained Glass, Cutting Tools and
Ceramic Kiln Fired Plates

B & B Products
Etchall
18700 N. 107th Avenue #13
Sun City, AZ 85373-9759
TEL: 1-888-382-4255/1-888-ETCH-ALL
www.etchall.com
Etchall etching products which
produce permanent etching finishes on
glass, ceramic, porcelain and slate

willow and coppice wood

The Country Seat, Inc.
1013 Old Philly Pike
Kepmton, PA 19529
TEL: 610-756-6124
www.countryseat.com

Restoration Products
3191 West 975 South
Fairmount, IN 46928
TEL: 1-800-562-5291
www.basketry.com

Wood N' Baskets
945 Pauline Avenue
Pine City, NY 14871
www.woodnbaskets.com

V.I. Reed & Cane, Supplies & Kits
Route 5
Box 632
Rogers, AR 72756
TEL: 1-800-852-0025
www.basketweaving.com

mosaic

Mountaintop Mosaics
Elm Street

P.O. Box 653
Castleton, VT 05735
TEL: 1-800-564-4980
www.mou
topmosaics.com
Vitreous Glass and Smalti Mosaic Tiles

Norberry Tile
207 Second Avenue South
Seattle, WA 98104
TEL: 206-343-9916
www.norberrytile.com
Mosaic Arts And Crafts - Distributors
of Ceramic, Glass,
and Stone Tile

Wits End Mosaic
P. O. Box 636
Sanford, FL 32772-0636
TEL: 407-323-9122
www.mosaic-witsend.com
Mosaic tiles, tools and other
supplies

wood

Art & Woodcrafters Supply
671 Highway 165 at Coffelt County
Branson, MO 65616
TEL: 417-335-8382
www.artwoodcrafter.com
Woodcrafter Supplies

Carpenter's Shoppe
3501 S. Norton Avenue
Sioux Falls, SD 57105
TEL: 605-336-0616
www.siteleader.com/catalogdepot/
TCSC-home
Unfinished Wood Craft Supplies

Wood N' Crafts
P. O. Box 140
Lakeview, MI 48850
TEL: 1-800-444-8075
www.wood-n-crafts.com
Wholesale Crafts Supplies

Wood & Shop, Inc.
5605 North Lindburgh
St. Louis, MO 63042
TEL: 314-731-2761
www.woodnshop.com
Hardwoods and wood cutting
supplies

Woodcraft Supply Corporation
4420 Emerson Avenue

Parkersburg, WV 26104
TEL: 304-485-4050
Locations Throughout
The United States
www.woodcraft.com
Woodworking tools

Woodcrafts & Supplies
405 East Indiana Street
Oblong, IL 62449
TEL: 1-800-592-4907
www.woodcraftssupplies.com
Woodworking Supplies and Tools

shells

A & J Shell Marine, Inc.
1165-A Revere Avenue
San Francisco, CA 94124
TEL: 415-822-7373
www.ajshellmarine.com
Wholesaler of sea shells for
craft work
Allen's Shell-a-rama

P.O. Box 72
Vallejo, CA 94590-6072
TEL: 707-554-9790
www.shellarama.com
Seashells and other Nautical Items
for Craftspeople

Shell Horizons
14191 63rd Way
Clearwater, FL 33760
TEL: 727-536-3333
www.shellhorizons.com
Wholesaler of Seashells & Seashell
Products

major retailers

Restoration Hardware
1200 Morris Turnpike
Short Hills Shopping Mall
Short Hills, NJ
TEL: 973-912-7300
www.RestorationHardware.com
Locations Throughout

The United States
Home Base
2120 Barranca Parkway
Irvine, CA 92606
TEL: 949-752-2390
www.homebase.com
Locations Throughout
The United States

Home Depot
2450 Cumberland Parkway
Atlanta, GA 30339
TEL: 770-432-9930
www.homedepot.com
Locations Throughout
The United States

Loew's Home Improvement
Warehouse
2003 US Highway 421
Wilkesboro, NC 28697
TEL: 336-838-1500
www.lowes.com
Locations Throughout
The United States

index

dedication For my mother, Jean

author's acknowledgments Firstly I would like to thank all the makers who have so generously given their time and expertise to make this book what it is. I would also like to thank Rosemary Hill for her encouragement and wise counsel; Jill Chisholm for her unwavering friendship; David Cox for the photograph of me; my friends and colleagues at *Crafts* magazine for their patience and support; and finally Stuart Cooper, my commissioning editor, who gave me the opportunity to write this book.

publisher's acknowledgments

The Publisher would like to thank the following photographers and organizations for permission to reproduce the photographs in this book: 1 Shannon Tofts (Artist: Lizzie Farey); 2–3 Michele Lamontagne/Cords sur Ciel, France; 7 Melanie Eclare/Maat Llewellyn's Garden (design: Ivan Hicks); 8 Jacqui Hurst; 9 Helen Fickling/Interior Archive; 10 by permission of The British Library/Flemish illustration from La Roman de la Rose; 11 Andrew Lawson; 12 Christian Sarramon; 13 left Richard Felber; 13 right Gary Rogers; 14 left Clive Nichols (design: Jan Truman CSMA Garden/RHS Hampton Court); 14 right Richard Felber; 15 Gary Rogers; 16 left Marijke Heuff; 16 right Clay Perry/The Garden Picture Library; 17 James Merrell/Country Homes and Interiors/Robert Harding Syndication; 18–19 Helen Fickling (location: Natalie Bell/design: Rene Slee); 20 left Mark Bolton (garden design: Duncan Skene, Somerset-bird by Neil Pickering); 20 right Andrew Lawson (Sculptor: Sophie Thompson); 20 below Chris Potter/Bradley Gardens, Northumberland (design: Andy McDermott); 21 left Jacqui Hurst (Sculptor: Barbara Hurst); 21 right Jacqui Hurst (Sculptor: Rupert Till); 31 Andrew Lawson (design: Ivan Hicks); 32 Bridgeman Art Library (Cotehele House, Cornwall); 33 Ronald Sheridan/Ancient Art & Architecture Collection (Canterbury Cathedral); 34 left Gary Rogers; 34–35 main picture Edifice/Lewis; 36 Edifice/Darley; 37 left Anne Smyth/Crafts Council; 37 right D. Pearl/Crafts Council; 38 Sculpture by Peter Layton – Glass Maker, London; 38–39 main picture Andrew Lawson (Stone Lane Gardens, Chagford, Devon); 39 right Glass sculpture by George Erml; 40 Sandy Schofield Fine Art; 41 left Michael Blake/The Coach-house Garden, Dublin Castle (Sculptor: Killian Schurman); 41 right J S Sira/The Garden Picture Library (Kew Gardens); 42 above left Peter Freeman; 42 right Clive Nichols/Garden & Security Lighting; 42 below left Clive Nichols (design: Jonathan Ballie); 43 left Clive Nichols/CSMA Garden/RHS Hampton Court (design: Jan Truman); 43 right Richard Felber; 53 Jerome Darblay/Inside; 54 Bibliothèque Nationale, Paris (MS Arsenal 5070,f.168); 55–56 Gary Rogers; 57 Edifice/Lewis; 58 Gary Rogers (design: Mark Anthony Walker); 59 left Clive Nichols/Parnham House Garden, Dorset (carved crocodile by Jerry Burgess); 60 Richard Felber; 61 Michele Lamontagne; 62 left Marianne Majerus (design: George Carter); 62–63 centre Richard Felber; 63 right Richard Felber; 64 left John Glover/RHS Chelsea (design: Julie Toll); 64 right Andrew Lawson (design: Paul Anderson); 65 above left Marijke Heuff/The Garden Picture Library; 65 above right Bench sculpture by Peter Adams, Australia; 65 below Nicola Browne (design: Clive West and Johnny Woodford); 74 Jacqui Hurst; 75 Sunniva Harte; 76 The British Architectural Library/RIBA London; 77–78 Andrew Lawson; 79 Juliette Wade/Priory d'Orsan, France; 80 left Andrew Lawson/Stone Lane Gardens, Chagford, Devon; 80 right Andrew Lawson/Roche Court, Wiltshire; 81 Jill Billington/Yorkshire Sculpture Park (Sculpture by Patrick Dougherty); 82 left J C Mayer – G Le Scanff; 82 right Jacqui Hurst (design: Serena de la Hey); 83 Ray Main; 84–85 main picture John de Visser; 85 above right & below right Richard Felber; 86 left Michele Lamontagne (Festival des Jardins de Chaumont-sur-Loire, (41) France); 86 right John de Visser; 87 above left Brigitte Perdereau (Festival des Jardins de Chaumont-sur-Loire, (41) France); 87 above right John de Visser; 87 below Richard Felber; 97 Rebecca Newnham Mosaics; 98 Erich Lessing/AKG; 99 left Erich Lessing/AKG; 99 right Marion Nickig/Quinta da Regaleira, Portugal; 100 Erica Craddock/The Garden Picture Library/Parc Guell, Barcelona; 101 Deidi von Schaewen/Parc Guell, Barcelona, Spain; 102 Jerry Harpur (design: Phillip Watson, Virginia); 103 Andrew Lawson (design: Margot Knox); 104 Richard Felber; 105 left Helen Fickling (location: Natalie Bell/design: Kate Otten); 105 right Helen Fickling/The Interior Archive/Maison Picassette, Chartres, France; 106 left Marianne Majerus/Groombridge Place (design: Ivan Hicks); 106 right Jerry Harpur (design: Bob Clark); 107 Jacqui Hurst (design: Cleo Mussi); 108 left design:Cleo Mussi/ stairwell for Colchester Hospital; 108 right Deidi von Schaewen; 109 above left Helen Fickling/Interior Archive/Maison Picassette, Chartres, France; 109 above right Mark Whitfield (Mosaic by Andrea Peters/The Pea-Green Pottery,Islington,London); 109 below Andrea Jones/Children's Playground, Showakinen Memorial Park, Nr. Tokyo, Japan (design: Fumiaki Takano); 120 left Nicholas Tosi/Stylist: Bernard Houillat/Marie Claire Maison; 120–121 main picture Simon Upton/ World of Interiors/The Condé Nast Publications Ltd; 121 right Edifice/Keate; 122 Simon McBride; 123 Michele Lamontagne; 124 Jacqui Hurst (design: Joe Smith); 125 left Mark Bolton/Mr and Mrs John Bracey, 'Scypen', South Devon; 125 right Brigitte Perdereau; 126 left Andrew Lawson/Stone Lane Gardens, Chagford, Devon; 126 right Andrea Jones/Showakinen Memorial Park, Nr. Tokyo, Japan (design: Fumiaki Takano); 127 Michele Lamontagne/Festival des Jardins de Chaumont-sur-Loire, (41) France; 128 left Marianne Majerus (design: Marc Schoellen); 128 right Gardens Illustrated/Melanie Eclare (Ballymaloe Cookery School); 129 Marianne Majerus (design: Emma Stabler); 130 above left J C Mayer – G Le Scanff/Festival des Jardins de Chaumont-sur-Loire, (41) France (design: Thomas Boog & Patrick Bailly); 130 below left Marianne Majerus (design: George Carter); 130–131 main picture Jackie Townsend/ Insight Picture Library (Design: Daniel Harvey); 131 above right Helen Fickling/Festival des Jardins de Chaumont-sur-Loire, (41) France; 131 below right Clive Nichols/RHS Chelsea (design: Julie Toll); 131 far right Michele Lamontagne/Festival des Jardins de Chaumont-sur-Loire, (41) France. Thanks also to Mrs June Fawcett and Mrs Imogen Luxmore for allowing us to photograph in their gardens.

published by

The Lyons Press, 123 West 18th Street, New York, NY 10011
www.lyonspress.com

ISBN 1 585 740551

Text copyright © Geraldine Rudge 1999, Design and layout copyright © Conran Octopus Ltd 1999, Special photography copyright © Jacqui Hurst 1999

Commissioning Editor Stuart Cooper
Managing Editor Kate Bell
Copy Editors Jane Simmonds, Rachel Hagan
Editorial Assistant Alexandra Kent
Index Hilary Bird

Art Editor Isabel de Cordova
Picture Research Claire Taylor
Production Oliver Jeffreys

British Library Cataloguing-in-Publication Data. A catalogue record for this book is available from the British Library.

Colour origination by Sang Choy International, Singapore. Printed in China.